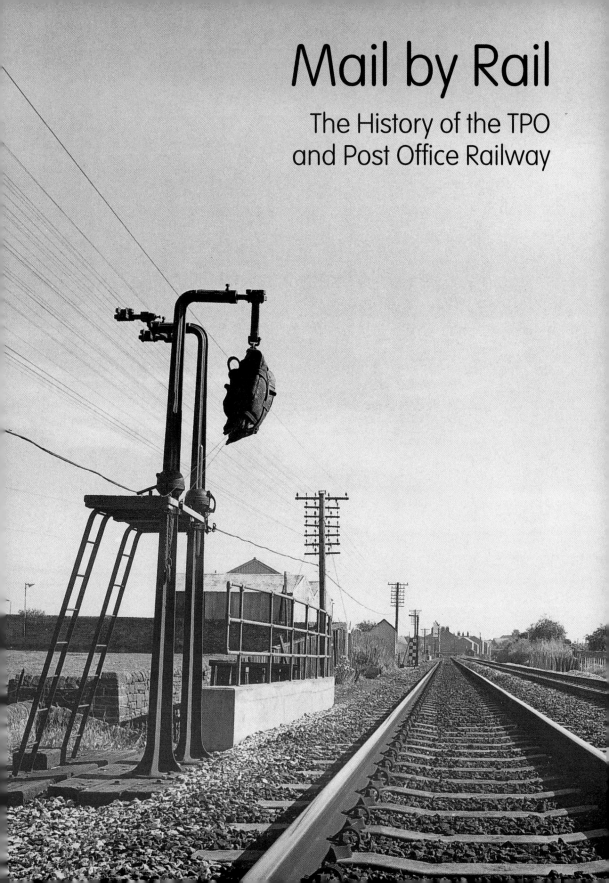

Mail by Rail

The History of the TPO
and Post Office Railway

Mail by Rail

The History of the TPO and Post Office Railway

PETER JOHNSON

IAN ALLAN
Publishing

First published 1995
Being a revised and updated edition of
The British Travelling Post Office first published in 1985.

ISBN 0 7110 2385 9

Published by Ian Allan Publishing

an imprint of Ian Allan Ltd, Terminal House,
Station Approach, Shepperton, Surrey TW17 8AS.
Printed by Ian Allan Printing Ltd, Coombelands House,
Coombelands Lane, Addlestone, Surrey KT15 1HY.

Front cover:
Top left: **Interior of a TPO.** *Brian Morrison*

Bottom left: **LMS stowage van No 3275.**
Peter Johnson Collection

Centre: **Royal Mail logo incorporating the
English crown.** *Brian Morrison*

Top right: **Preserved GWR stowage van
No 814 and lineside apparatus at Didcot.**
Author

Bottom right: **Attaching the pouch.**
H. Lazenby/Real Photographs

Back cover:
Top: **The Crewe-Bangor TPO waits to leave
Crewe on 17 March 1964.** *John Clarke*

Bottom: **Class 302 No 302 993 in Royal Mail
livery.** *Brian Morrison*

Contents

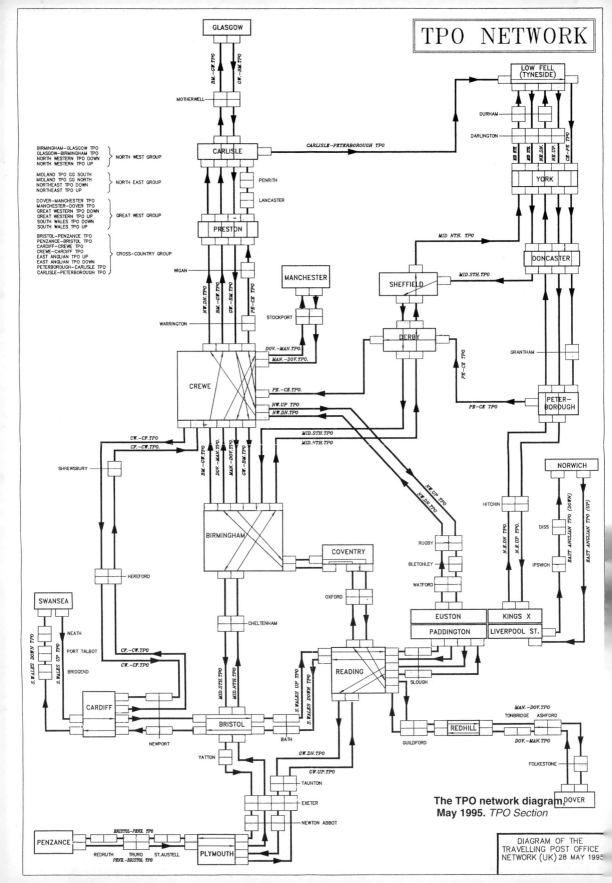

TPO NETWORK

The TPO network diagram
May 1995. *TPO Section*

DIAGRAM OF THE
TRAVELLING POST OFFICE
NETWORK (UK) 28 MAY 1995

Introduction

From the railways' earliest days there have been links with the carriage of mail, officially first with the opening of the Liverpool & Manchester Railway in 1830, when bagged mail was carried. This relationship has developed and even in the mid-1990s continues to flourish, despite the competing attractions of internal air and road transport. With some exceptions, referred to later, this alliance has had a very low profile; indeed, it is only since 1990 that Travelling Post Office carriages have carried branding enabling the public to know their purpose.

For many, railway enthusiasts and others, the Travelling Post Offices are something of an enigma. A good number of them will recall that most famous of documentaries, *Night Mail*, now regularly shown on television and amongst enthusiasts' gatherings. Others, when faced with a sorting carriage at a British Rail depot open day, will declaim that 'this is what used to be', disbelieving that sorting letters on trains that run at night is just as much a feature of late 20th century postal and railway operation as it was in the 19th century. A late-night rail traveller catching a glimpse through the open doors of a TPO whilst loading or unloading takes place at a major station is similarly likely to be disbelieving. Likewise, most of those who clamour to watch the apparatus demonstrations at Didcot and Quorn are probably unaware of the continued operation of Travelling Post Offices. Indeed, it cannot be surprising that, by their very nature, Travelling Post Offices remain unknown to the majority of the population.

But the TPOs are not the only link between the Royal Mail and the railways, or indeed, with railway operation. An innovation for the 1990s is the development of Railnet, a £150 million project which will link road, rail and air to speed up mail handling and improve the reliability of mail services. Of particular interest here are the 16 dual-voltage four-car trains built for the Royal Mail to carry mail in containers over the electric rail network. This new stock demonstrates a major change in philosophy, for whilst the traditional TPOs were built and operated to Post Office requirements but owned by the railway companies, the new trains are owned by the Royal Mail.

Below: **This rather spacious impression of TPO working dates to 1865. Probably representing the North Western TPO (Night Down) it is notable for showing the off-centre corridor connection and vents for the oil lamps.** *London Journal*

If the Travelling Post Offices barely scratch the surface of the public conscience it can hardly be surprising that the Royal Mail's own underground railway is scarcely known at all. Designed and started before World War 1 and completed nearly 10 years after the war was over, this 2ft gauge line runs under the centre of London, from Paddington to the Eastern District Sorting Office, carrying millions of letters and keeping them off the capital's busy streets, with almost no sign of its existence showing above the surface, unlike London's other Underground. Now called Rail Mail, the Post Office Railway has done much to minimise the level of traffic on London's streets and deserves to be more widely known.

Collectors and enthusiasts have for a long time been interested in the TPOs; the former because of the distinctive datestamps allocated to them, perpetuating the names of long-defunct railway companies, the latter because of the non-standard rolling stock, for many years restricted to night-time operation, and that 'star' of *Night Mail*, the apparatus. The Post Office Railway usually makes its presence known with its anniversaries, celebrating its 21st in 1948 and then at 10-year intervals since its 40th in 1967; philatelic souvenirs, or even publicly advertised visits, have been arranged. The Railnet stock probably will not have the same attraction but it will keep the Royal Mail on the rails well into the next century. It is appropriate, then, that these three strands should be brought together for consideration in this book, as mail by rail.

Acknowledgements

In the 10 years since *The British Travelling Post Office* was published I have been pleased to acquire new information on British TPOs, much of it from readers of that book, previously unknown to me. Frank Scheer, an American expert on mail transmission the world over, so keen he got a senior job with the US Postal Service, was the first, and showed the way to *The Traveller*, a little-known magazine produced by TPO staff for themselves. Others were C. E. F. Moss, who wrote about the last use of apparatus and the final days of 70294; M. S. King, who provided data on the TPOs of the Southern Railway and its constituents; Jeremy Clarke proved knowledgeable about the Mk 1 stock; and Colin Flint and Brian White, both former stalwarts of the Peterborough-Crewe TPO, where I first met them, provided insights into the 'traveller's' life; Brian kindly found the time to comment on the script. Alan Violet, my long-time friend and colleague of the Railway Philatelic Group, was the source of the illustration of 'apparatus working' with a horse-drawn mail coach.

Harold Wilson continues to lead the way in researching TPO history, especially from the philatelic side; neither of these books could have been written without his pioneering efforts. His own masterwork on TPOs should be on the shelves before too much longer.

Chris Whitehead was kind enough to lend material from his collection and John Bailey was equally kind enough to give me his late father's, Paul Bailey's, TPO file, which in turn contained the results of the late W. G. Stitt Dibden's researches into early TPO history; I quite often spent time talking trains and collecting with Paul when he should have been marrying someone in the Superintendent Registrar's office he ran.

The 814 team at Didcot made me welcome and allowed me to see the apparatus from the inside, with a generous offer to train me how to work it in the future.

This is one of many books which would be much poorer were it not for F. W. 'Tim' Shuttleworth's efforts in the darkroom; I am equally grateful to Paul Rees for providing repro services without demur or question.

Against all the odds, the University of Leicester Library came up with a description of TPO working of 1839 which also served to establish the credentials of two old engravings. The Royal Mail's own archives, too, are a goldmine well worth excavating.

Since 1984 I have had the pleasure of meeting many TPO personnel and without exception have found them courteous and co-operative to the enthusiastic observer of their activities. Norman Peachell, the Manager, TPOs I met on the Whitehaven-Huddersfield in 1985; Dick Escudier, with whom I travelled to Carlisle in 1988; Richard Yeo, who many will have met on TPOs at BR open days; Brian Collett and Clive Brooks, of TPO section; Alex Obradovic, my anonymous guide to TPOs in 1984 who kindly passed on the results of his own researches and who arranged a display sorting carriage for the Railway Philatelic Group's 25th anniversary in 1991; Willie McCoombe, the inspector who gave me his TPO tie; Ken Redpath, who was i/c when I travelled on the North Eastern; Brian Quinn, the current Manager, TPOs; these are the names I know.

On the Post Office Railway Engineering Manager Colin Tipp and Duty PHG David Kemp graciously answered my questions and showed me round Mount Pleasant at very short notice.

All these, and others whose names I didn't discover, have made a valuable contribution to this book and I thank them most sincerely. Any errors remaining are my own responsibility.

Peter Johnson
Leicester
June 1995

Any reader interested in keeping up to date on the TPOs should consider joining the Railway Philatelic Group. For details send a self-addressed stamped envelope to the Membership Secretary at 12 Maplewell Drive, Leicester LE4 1BD.

1. The Travelling Post Office

Prior to the introduction of the railways, mail handling in the UK was slow and often unreliable. The Romans had introduced a postal system of considerable complexity and efficiency but it rapidly disappeared when the empire collapsed. Medieval monarchs and governments took little or no interest in the provision of private communications, often leaving it to business interests to develop their own systems. It was only with the coming of the Renaissance that governments began to take a positive interest in developing communications over and above those required for their own needs. During the reign of Queen Elizabeth I private persons were allowed to use the system set up for the transmission of state papers between London and Dublin.

In 1635 a royal proclamation reorganised the inland service in an attempt to make the carriage of mails self-sufficient, as the royal purse was finding the costs

incurred a burden. It was decreed that the posts should cover at least 120 miles per day. Where a post existed, the public was not allowed to use alternatives. Despite this regulation it was not until 1657 that an Act of Parliament was enacted establishing the government's monopoly and the position of Postmaster-General. At this time mails were being carried by stage coaches at considerably less speed than the earlier scheme for state papers. For example, in 1706 a London (the Black Swan, Holborn)-York (also the Black Swan, in Coney Street) stage coach service was announced to take four days, 'if God permits'; the service was to run three days per week, leaving at 5.00am. To travel by stage coach must have been an awesome experience; the roads were atrocious and the coaches often broke down because they had no springs. It is recorded that the rough riding of the vehicles often made passengers ill.

Improvements were not to come about until the passing of the Roads Acts, permitting the construction and operation of toll roads, in the 18th century. Special coaches for the mails, accompanied by armed guards, commenced in 1784. These speeded up the mails considerably and London to Holyhead was reduced to 36hr and accommodation was also provided for five passengers. This phase reached its peak in the earlier part of the 19th century, with the great trunk roads built by McAdam, Telford and others. In 1837, 27 mail coaches left London nightly.

The 1825 opening of the Stockton & Darlington Railway had no influence on the carriage of mails, although it is said that letters with string tied around them were carried as parcels, to circumvent the General Post Office's monopoly. The railway's comparatively isolated situation did not put it in the position of being a forerunner in this instance.

A completely different situation arose with the opening of the Liverpool & Manchester Railway five years later. For one thing the L&MR connected a large developing port with a similar industrial centre and there were parties at either end who wished to communicate and transport goods. By the end of 1830

Left: **Transmission of time; the TPO supervisor hands the official watch to a postman at Holyhead.** *Real Photos*

9

traffic was such that Liverpool & Manchester Railway carriages *Wellington* and *Lord Derby* had been adapted to carry bagged mail, followed by *Fly* the following year.

There were to be no further developments in mail transmission until the Grand Junction Railway opened from Birmingham to Warrington on 4 July 1837. Mails were carried from the opening but between London and Birmingham they were still carried by road, the journey time from London to Liverpool being 16hr. The GPO commenced negotiating with the company for terms and conditions under which the service could be expanded. Considering the company's terms too expensive it tried to obtain powers from Parliament which would apply to all railway companies. Had the GPO succeeded it would have gained complete control over the operation of the railways. Clauses in the Bill required the railways to provide, at their own cost:

'Carriages and locomotives, special, ordinary, or otherwise, to carry the mails at all hours of the day or night, at such speed, and stopping at such places and just so long as the Postmaster-General shall provide.

'Replace, at their own cost, any carriages provided by them and rejected by the Postmaster-General, for any duty.

'Give precedence to postal requirements, over and above the requirements of fare-paying passengers.

'Obey the Postmaster-General's orders respecting the conveyance, delivery, and leaving of the mails, and the place the Post Office carriage shall have in the train.'

Further, it allowed the Post Office:

'If running its own trains, to do so without payment of any rate or tolls whatsoever. To remove all obstructions to their locos. To use anything, locos, carriages, ropes, etc, of the company on every part of the line, to work their engines for carrying the mails, and passengers.

'To repudiate any by-laws contradictory to its powers.

'To inflict a penalty for disobedience of any of its orders.

'To alter or rescind any of its contracts with the companies, by three months' notice, or without, the companies not to have similar powers.'

Obviously the companies petitioned against the Bill, for the resulting Act was more acceptable to them. Despite this the GPO still had wide-ranging powers; it could put mails on any train; it could demand special trains at its convenience; it could ask the companies not to change the time of certain trains without notifying the Post Office; and it could ask for the provision of special rolling stock.

Payments for the use of the trains commenced at £1,743 in 1838, had increased to £490,223 in 1860 and

in 1896 had reached £1 million, an ample demonstration of the growth of both rail and postal systems. The idea that mail could be sorted on the move first came to the fore in January 1838. It originated with Fredrick Karstadt, a Post Office surveyor, who saw a way of reducing some of the paperwork that applied with the system already used. It was agreed to run an experimental service, employing Karstadt's son and another as mail clerks. The Grand Junction Railway provided a converted horsebox for the purpose of the experiment and the service started on 20 January 1838. Coincidentally a letter addressed to the Chairman of the Grand Junction Railway at Liverpool and written on that first run came to public notice 150 years later. On the envelope the writer recorded that the train was moving at 'the rate of 26 miles an hour', with the speed underlined, and that it was the second letter written in 'a moving Post Office drawn by locomotive power', the first having been addressed to the Postmaster-General.

The experiment was an immediate success and, on 28 May 1838, the railway company was asked to provide a permanent sorting carriage. This would bring the operation on the Grand Junction in line with the one recently started on the London & Birmingham Railway.

On 9 April 1838 the London & Birmingham Railway extended its Euston line from Tring to Denbigh Hall and opened its line between Rugby and Birmingham. The construction of the Kilsby Tunnel was to delay the opening of the line throughout until August. Purpose-built sorting carriages were put into service on the opened sections on 22 May. A contract authorising this and agreeing to the carriage of mail on ordinary trains was signed a week later. In November 1839 *The Literary World* described the carriage as 'fitted internally with nests of "pigeon holes", drawers, desks and pegs'. Staffing was by 'one or more clerks and a guard; the former to sort and arrange letters, during the journey, and the latter to tie up and exchange the mail bags'. The journey time was 5hr for the day mail, 5½ for the night.

The North Union Railway was opened between Wigan and Preston on 7 November 1838. The GPO was quick to take advantage of the 225-mile length of railway thus created by amalgamating and extending the London & Birmingham and the Grand Junction Railway post offices the same day. Within a week, for reasons unknown, the service was known as the Grand Northern Railway Post Office.

From 20 January 1839 the day mail used a single sorting carriage, and first-class passengers were also carried. The night mail used a sorting carriage and a letter bag carriage. Extended to Lancaster following the opening of the Lancaster & Preston Junction Railway on 26 June 1840, in 1841 the mail was reported, in *The Penny Magazine*, as taking 11hr for the 241 miles, including a half hour stop at Birmingham. Scottish mails were taken forward by

Above: **The interior of the replica 1838 coach built by the LMS for the TPO centenary in 1938. The photograph was taken during the exhibition held at Euston.** *GPO Newsroom*

mail coaches. These services were the forerunners of the famous Down and Up Special Travelling Post Offices.

The public sometimes felt that the GPO was not always so quick to take advantage of new routes to improve its services, however, for in 1840, in anticipation of the opening of the North Midland Railway from Derby to Masbrough, the *Sheffield Mercury* was complaining that the London mails were still being routed via Birmingham and, at 14hr, were taking 3hr longer than via Derby. The paper explained that the direct route entailed leaving Euston Square at 6.00am and changing at Derby to a four-horse coach to complete the journey. Meanwhile, the mail was leaving Euston Square at 8.30pm for Birmingham, doubling back to Hampton-in-Arden before continuing to Derby as before. It called upon the towns served by the North Midland Railway to press the Postmaster-General for a direct service. A branch mail, from Rugby to Darlington, had been established by 1841.

Although of a later date, a contract entered into between the GPO and the Great Northern Railway in 1883 contained, *inter alia*, the following clauses, which may be considered typical:

'12 The Company shall provide and run as and when required by the Postmaster-General or the Inspector-General of Mails for the time being on all or any of the Trains specified in the 1st 2nd and 3rd Schedules (except the Day Mail Train between Grantham and Nottingham specified in the 2nd Schedule) one Sorting Van or one Mail Tender or other suitable Vehicle of such special pattern as may be required by the Postmaster-General on each such Train Provided that if at any time the Company shall cease to run any of the Trains specified in the 3rd Schedule by which Sorting Vans or Mail Tenders may be conveyed under this Contract or shall run any of such Trains at hours which will be unsuitable for the Mail Service the Postmaster-General shall have the power to require the Company to provide and run on any other Train of the Company the Sorting Vans or Mail Tenders which have theretofore been provided and run on

11

Left: **LMS sorting carriage No 30204 was built at Wolverton in 1934. It was a 57ft vehicle which later achieved unwanted notoriety by being on the Up Special TPO on 7 August 1963, the victim of the Great Train Robbery. No 30204 never ran in the Up Special again, being transferred to the Manchester-Glasgow SC; later it was scrapped by King's of Norwich, the body being burnt at Wymondham and the frame and bogies cut up at Trowse.**
Peter Johnson Collection

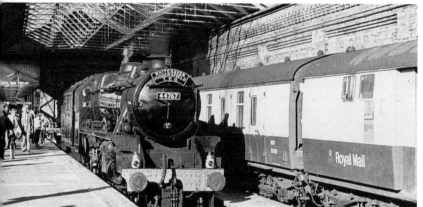

Left: **Class 5 4-6-0 No 44767 *George Stephenson* at Workington prior to working the Whitehaven-Huddersfield TPO on 6 September 1985.**
Peter Johnson

Left: **Class 47 No 47515 was named *Night Mail* at Derby on 26 September 1986 to commemorate the 50th anniversary of the famous film. The ceremony was performed by the Managing Director, Royal Mail Letters, Bill Cockburn.**
Peter Johnson

the trains so discontinued or run at unsuitable hours as aforesaid.

'13 All Sorting Carriages Mail Tenders or other Vehicles and all lamps required for the purposes of the Post Office under this Contract shall be of such size and pattern and be in all respects so built constructed and fitted up as the Postmaster-General or the Inspector-General of Mails shall reasonably require, and shall be provided and furnished and kept in good safe and sufficient repair and replaced when necessary (by Carriages or Lamps either of the same or any other pattern) at the cost of the Company and to the approval of the Postmaster-General or the Inspector-General of Mails.

'14 All sorting Carriages Mail Tenders or other Vehicles and Lamps used for the purposes of the Post Office Mail Service under this Contract and which may be in such use when the new midday Mail Services specified in the first part of Schedule 2 commence shall be considered as having been approved by the Postmaster-General and in case any alterations (not being repairs required under the last preceding Clause) for Post Office purposes shall at any time thereafter be required by the Postmaster-General or Inspector-General of Mails in any such Carriages Mail Tenders or other Vehicles or Lamps or in any other Carriages Mail Tenders Vehicles or Lamps which the Postmaster-General shall have approved of such alterations shall be made by the Company and the actual cost thereof paid by the Postmaster-General.'

The contract contained 24 clauses and three schedules; by 1895 a contract with the Lancashire & Yorkshire Railway and the LNWR, jointly, for the 'conveyance of Her Majesty's mails over the Preston and Wyre and Preston and Longridge Railways' had been simplified to 14 clauses and one schedule.

An interesting feature of mail handling on the first TPOs concerned bags destined for minor stations at which the train was not due to stop. They were thrown on to the platform as the train passed through! Even at 25mph considerable damage could be done, both to the mails and any innocent bystander! Clearly something would have to be done to improve the situation. The solution probably originated from mail coach practice, for in some locations mail bags were not only thrown from a moving coach, they were also picked up on the move, by being hung from a post for the mail guard to grasp as the coach passed by.

It was Nathaniel Worsdell who designed and built the first apparatus for exchanging mail bags with a moving train. He was the Superintendent of the Grand Junction Railway's carriage works and helped his father build the *Rocket*'s tender in 1829; later his sons made names for themselves on the North Eastern Railway. Worsdell had built and tested his apparatus in 1837, and was granted a provisional patent for it on 4 January 1838, before even the first sorting carriage

had run. Worsdell was aware of the damage being done to mail and personnel by the initial arrangements and would have had no difficulty in seeing the need for some sort of apparatus. Following tests at Winsford, Cheshire, the GPO sought to make use of the equipment but failed to agree a price with Worsdell, who was never to profit from his invention.

The Post Office still wished to use such a device, so encouraged one of its employees, John Ramsey, to investigate the matter. Ramsey devised an apparatus which was tested successfully at Boxmoor on 30 May 1838. This was two days after the Post Office had notified Worsdell that his final offer had been refused!

The *Literary Review* described the operation of Ramsey's apparatus thus: 'For taking and delivering the bags, during the passage of the train, to obviate stoppages for this purpose, attached to the near side of the office is an iron frame, with a piece of net, which is extended to receive a bag from the arm of a standard at the side of the road. At the same moment that a bag is delivered into the net, another is let down from the office by the machine, and thus an exchange of bags is instantly effected.'

In addition to the installation at Boxmoor, apparatus was installed at Leighton Buzzard and Berkhamsted, all three sites being brought into regular use on 27 October 1838. From 5 March 1839 further apparatus sites at Bletchley, Weedon, Bescot, Penkridge, Winsford and Preston Brook were brought into use. Despite the initial success of Ramsey's apparatus, further installations over the next two years encountered considerable difficulties. It appears that the rather complicated apparatus worked satisfactorily under test conditions, but did not stand up to normal wear and tear. Also, little provision had been made for the capture of bags dropped off the TPOs, strong winds sometimes causing the bags to be blown under the train. Further experiments included weighting the bags with lead shot.

An inspector called Dicker, who was in charge of the ground installations, made many modifications and improvements, even going to the extent of building working models in his own time and at his own expense. His efforts were rewarded on 15 April 1848 when he was able to try an apparatus of his own devising at Croydon. On 1 September 1848 Dicker's apparatus was also brought into use at Edenbridge and New Cross. It worked to everyone's satisfaction and was accepted for use by the GPO. There was, however, a sting in the tail of this acceptance: it was considered possible that Dicker's apparatus might infringe Worsdell's patent so its introduction was delayed on the LNWR until 1852, when the patent expired. Dicker did eventually receive £500 for his trouble and his device was to remain in use, with little modification, for more than 100 years. At its peak, before World War 1, 245 sets had been installed at 220 locations. Under the GPO's supervision and instruction the railway companies were paid for

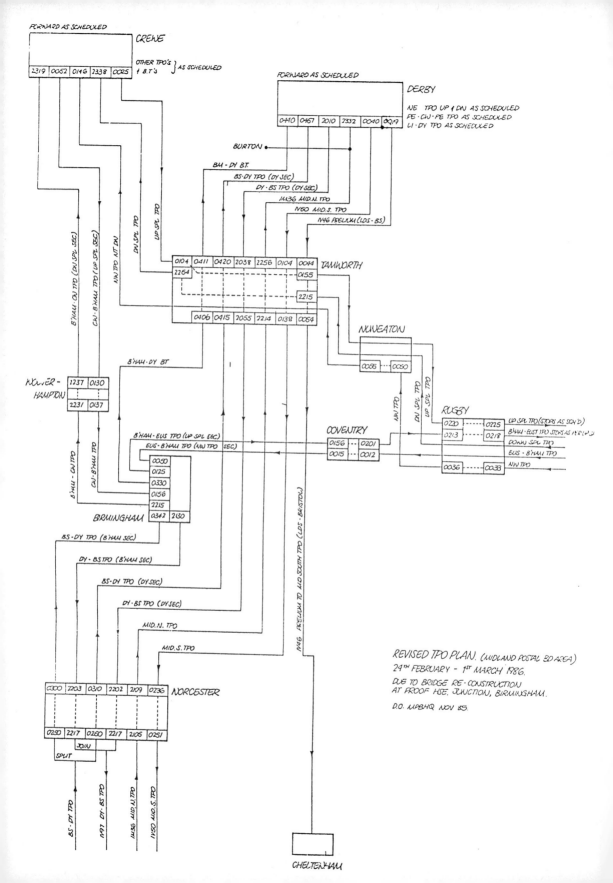

FORWARD AS SCHEDULED

CREWE

| 2319 | 0052 | 0146 | 2338 | 0025 |

OTHER TPO's } AS SCHEDULED
& B.T's

FORWARD AS SCHEDULED

DERBY

| 0440 | 0457 | 2010 | 7332 | 0040 | 0019 |

NE · TPO UP & DN · AS SCHEDULED
PE · CW · PE TPO AS SCHEDULED
LI · DY TPO AS SCHEDULED

BURTON

BU · DY BT.
BS·DY TPO (DY SEC)
DY · BS TPO (DY SEC)
M36 MID.N. TPO
N50 MID.S. TPO
N46 PRELIM (LDS · BS)

0104	0411	0420	2038	2256	0104	0044	TAMWORTH
2264						0155
						2215
0406	0415	2055	2214	0138	0054

B'HAM · DN TPO (DN SPL SEC)
CW · B'HAM TPO (UP SPL SEC)
NN TPO KIT DN
DN SPL TPO
UP SPL TPO

NUNEATON

| 0055 | 0050 |

WOLVER-
HAMPTON

| 1237 | 0130 |
| 2231 | 0137 |

B'HAM · DY BT

NN TPO
DN SPL TPO
UP SPL TPO

RUGBY

| 0220 | 0225 | UP SPL TPO (STOPS AS SCH'D)
| 0213 | 0218 | B'HAM · EUST TPO STOPS AS PER (?)
| | | DOWN SPL TPO
| | | EUS · B'HAM TPO
| 0036 | 0033 | NN TPO

COVENTRY

| 0156 | 0201 |
| 0015 | 0012 |

B'HAM · EUS TPO (UP SPL SEC)
EUS · B'HAM TPO (NN TPO SEC)

BIRMINGHAM

| 0050 |
| 0125 |
| 0330 |
| 0156 |
| 2215 |
| 0342 | 2130 |

B'HAM · DN TPO
CW · B'HAM TPO

BS · DY TPO (B'HAM SEC)
DY · BS TPO (B'HAM SEC)
BS · DY TPO (DY SEC)
DY · BS TPO (DY SEC)
MID. N. TPO
MID. S. TPO

N46 PRELIM TO 440 SOUTH TPO (LDS · BRISTOL)

WORCESTER

| 0300 | 2203 | 0310 | 2202 | 2109 | 0236 |
| 0250 | 2217 | 0260 | 2217 | 2105 | 0251 |
| JOIN |
| SPLIT |

BS · DY TPO
M97 DY · BS TPO
M36 MID.N. TPO
N50 440 · S. TPO

REVISED TPO PLAN. (MIDLAND POSTAL BD AREA)
24TH FEBRUARY – 1ST MARCH 1986.
DUE TO BRIDGE RE · CONSTRUCTION
AT PROOF HSE. JUNCTION, BIRMINGHAM.

D.O. MPBHQ NOV 85.

CHELTENHAM

Left: **A diagram showing the revised postal arrangements to cover the Proof House bridge reconstruction in 1986.** *Peter Johnson Collection*

Above: **The aerial filming of *Night Mail II* took place on the Midland main line on 20 September 1986, the specially prepared train being seen here at Glendon North Junction. The carriages are Nos 80365, 80422, 80320, 80362, 80421, 80363 and brake 80868. The stock was Newcastle-based and normally worked on the North Eastern TPO.**
Post Office

maintaining the ground apparatus, the 1883 contract between the GPO and the Great Northern Railway covering the matter thus:

'15 The Company shall allow the Postmaster-General to fix and maintain or the Postmaster-General may at his option require the Company to fix and maintain at the costs and risk of the Postmaster-General at such places or points on any of the Company's lines of Railway or on the sides thereof comprised in this Contract and to such one or more of the Carriages conveying the Mails as the Postmaster-General or Inspector-General of Mails may deem necessary an apparatus for the purpose of exchanging the Mail Bags while the Trains are in progress provided that such apparatus shall not be fixed at any Station or place where its use might be dangerous to life or property.'

The apparatus did not meet with universal approval though, for the GWR, advised by Brunel that it could not be used with safety on express trains, refused to allow its use, holding out until 1858. Then the first GWR apparatus sites were at Cholsey, Maidenhead, Slough, Uffington and West Drayton.

Another type of apparatus was described in the 25 October 1856 issue of *Mechanics' Magazine*. It was invented by A. D. Lacy, of Knayton in Yorkshire, who had obtained a patent. It appeared to use the same apparatus for both collecting and dispatching, in a similar manner to that used for exchanging single-line tablets at speed. It is not known how long Mr Lacy pursued the marketing of his patent.

The original TPOs were known as railway post offices. From the 1860s some services were called sorting tenders. The reason for the distinction is unknown but it could be that the RPOs were controlled from Post Office HQ, while the STs were controlled by the postmasters of the towns they served. The sorting tenders became known as sorting carriages from 1904 and the title certainly ceased to have any operational significance after control of all services passed to the London Postal Region in the 1930s. From 1914 the RPOs were called railway sorting carriages, this title lasting until 1928 when they became Travelling Post Offices. Other mail services have been designated Sunday sorting tenders, district sorting carriages and bag tenders.

Sunday sorting tenders evolved as a scheme to reduce the number of staff on duty at the London Chief Office on Sundays. On Saturday nights mail from towns around London, which could not be sorted before the usual up working reached the capital, was put on a down duty for transferring to an up duty at a suitable distance away from London. Seven services started on 20 April 1850 when 23 fewer men were required at the London Chief Office the following day. Rowland Hill, whose ideas for postal reform led to the introduction of the Universal Penny Post and the 1d black postage stamp, recorded the event in his diary. The services were eventually merged with the district sorting carriages.

Following the establishment of the 10 London district sorting offices in 1857/8 nine district sorting carriages were introduced between 1857 and 1863. They worked in the same manner as the Sunday sorting tenders but sorted the mail to the London districts. They were withdrawn in 1869 because increased mail volumes justified the expense of increasing the sorting duties at the district offices, rather than the £8,000 annual cost of the district sorting carriages.

Until 1991, for a period around Christmas, the TPOs suspended their sorting activities and ran as bag tenders. In this guise they operated with a reduced staff, handling only bagged mail. From 1970 special rubber datestamps were issued, intended for internal documentation only. Other bag tenders ran all the year round, although not all used postal vehicles. Introduced in November 1973, the Preston-London bag tender existed to relieve the Up Special TPO of Datapost traffic, a guaranteed next-day delivery service; the service was withdrawn after 25 January 1991. The London-Norwich bag tender operated between 1948 and 1990 and was the return working of the Norwich-London TPO.

From 1860 the public were allowed to post letters on to the TPOs on payment of an extra fee in addition to the normal postage. This was called the late fee and in 1860 it was 2d, although there were some variations in different parts of the country — in the Post Office Directory for 1876 the entry for Lincoln included the following: 'By affixing two extra stamps letters may be posted up to 8.10pm at the Travelling Post Office at the Midland Station'. In 1880 the late fee was reduced to ½d and remained thus until 30 June 1969 when it was increased to 1d. When the currency was decimalised on 15 February 1971 the late fee was converted to ½p. It became 1p on 24 June 1974 and was abolished, for letters, on 27 September 1976. Letters are still accepted on the TPOs, although they must be prepaid at the first class rate and posted in the boxes provided. This service is little used, largely because of lack of publicity, but there are some,

including newspaper contributors, who find it worthwhile.

In the 1980s TPO staff noted an organisation using specially printed envelopes drawing attention to the fact that their mail was posted on a train. Possibly the largest use of the TPO service is made on Budget night; a number of City finance houses vie to get their analyses of the Chancellor's intentions into the post with same-day postmarks — the TPOs allow them to achieve their objective. Some London termini which originate TPOs have late letter boxes, which can only be used at certain times, for mail which will be sent by TPO. Similar boxes existed at Bournemouth, Newton Abbot and Newcastle until the late 1980s. A late posting box is to be provided at the Willesden Hub (*qv*); at the time of publication it was not known what late posting facilities, if any, were to be provided at the regional hubs. Prior to decimalisation another late fee, of 1s 6d, existed for registered and recorded delivery mail. Upon decimalisation the fee became 7½p, then 10p from 24 June 1974 and 11p from 16 September 1991 until abolished after 25 June 1993; what is now described as prepaid priority service mail is still accepted on TPOs.

Writing in 1890 W. M. Ackworth noted, in *Scottish Railways — their present position*:

'There was another thing which much impressed me on the Spey-side line, as it always does in every part of the Highlands, and that was the admirable postal connections. Imagine a mail leaving Aberdeen at 3.30 a.m., and picking up and putting down its bags all along the route — in order that the fishermen of the Banff coast may find their Edinburgh and Glasgow letters awaiting them when they come down to breakfast. Yet more remarkable, imagine that from Inverness to Wick, through that "desert of silence", as Mr Foxwell appropriately terms Caithness, the Highland Company hurries the mails faster than the Italian lines can convey the international special train to Brindisi, faster than the German and the Belgian Governments, with the assistance of the Chemin de fer du Nord, can forward their passengers from Aix to Calais. Till someone can point out a better, I shall venture to believe that the combined rail and steamboat mail services to the eastern coast, and to Skye and the Lewis, are unmatched in the world.

'That they do not pay directly may be taken for granted. The postal subsidy of the Great North is nearly £18,000 a year, while that of the Highland is no less than £55,000, and probably all the postage stamps used throughout their territory would not cover this sum. But for all that few would be so foolish as to grudge the money. The Postmaster-General, with his omnipresent mail bags, and his yet more obtrusive parcel-post hampers — I saw six huge ones landed from the Orkney steamer one evening last June — is a far more efficient representative of the central government than any

Secretary of State for Scotland, and is doing more to cement the Union than any Scottish Home Rule League can do to break it.'

Ackworth's enthusiasm arose because he was observing the benefits of the 1885 Scottish mails acceleration. An examination of the historical list which follows will reveal a number of changes which took place that year; they had far-reaching effects. The most important aspect was the introduction of the Special Mail between Euston and Aberdeen, supplementing the North Western and Caledonian TPOs. A number of other services were introduced or extended to connect with the 'Special' and the basic pattern of services which evolved on the West Coast route lasted until 14 May 1993. The 'Special' became the Up Special TPO and the North Western and Caledonian TPOs evolved to become the Down Special TPO. Between them they provided the most comprehensive TPO service in the country. The Up Special, for example, ran to 12 postal vehicles and also conveyed a Manchester-Birmingham BG (gangwayed full brake) from Crewe to Birmingham. On an average night in the 1980s 250,000 letters and packets were sorted, many hundreds of mail bags carried as stowage and 1,100 items of Datapost dealt with.

In 1936 the GPO's film unit made a film, *Night Mail*, a documentary which has become a classic still demanded by audiences everywhere. With some film maker's licence it told the story of a night on the Down Special. John Huntley records in *Railways on the Screen* (2nd edition, Ian Allan 1993) that the locations were Euston, Bletchley and Crewe, although Broad Street substituted for the latter in some scenes and that the TPO interiors were faked at the Film Unit's Blackheath studio. With a soundtrack by Benjamin Britten, the poem which accompanied the film introduced the then unknown W. H. Auden to a wider audience.

The TPO service celebrated its centenary in 1938 and efforts were made to see that the public knew all about it. On 28 March a commemorative banquet at Euston station included the Postmaster-General, the Lord Mayor of London and the Mayor of St Pancras amongst the guests. Before dining they examined an exhibition train of TPO rolling stock through the ages displayed in the station. The train consisted of the LMS-built replica 1838 Grand Junction Railway TPO coach, a West Coast Joint Stock TPO coach of 1885 and a contemporary LMS vehicle; both the replica and the WCJS vehicles are in the National collection and are displayed in the National Railway Museum at York. A demonstration of apparatus working was given, in the station (?!), and a viewing of *Night Mail* took place in the LMS Shareholders' Meeting Room. The Postmaster-General took advantage of the occasion to announce the ordering of six 'luxury' sorting carriages — features were to include electric tea urns and ovens, extra draught-proofing and noise reduction and interiors painted 'a special green to reduce eye strain'. The exhibition train was opened to the public from midday on 28 March until 2 April.

Also in 1938 the GPO commissioned the well-known Northampton-based model making firm of Bassett-Lowke to build a scale working model of the Up Special. Taking three months to build, the train had three sorting carriages, a stowage van and two brake vans. It was hauled by a 'Royal Scot' class loco, the entire train being 17ft long. The layout for the model was a circuit of 120ft. At a scale of ⅜in to 1ft, the model was finely detailed, both internally and

17

Left: **LNER 'A4' class 4-6-2** *Mallard* **at Marylebone prior to working the 'Postal Pullman' to Banbury on 9 May 1988 to launch a set of stamps, one of which commemorated the 50th anniversary of** *Mallard's* **record run and the 150th anniversary of TPOs.**
Peter Johnson

externally; the door of the clothes locker opened to reveal a coat hook! The model was electrically driven, with the exchange apparatus working automatically as the train ran round the track, and the warning bell ringing while the net was extended. The fate of the model is unknown.

Although some services were withdrawn because of staffing problems, TPO operation was not greatly affected by World War 1. The same could not be said with regard to World War 2. Then, all the TPOs were withdrawn by 21 September 1940, while the Up and Down Specials and the Great Western services continued to operate as bag tenders; a total of 55 men had worked on the London-based services by the end of hostilities. Sorting was resumed on these services on 1 October 1945 but late fee letters were not allowed until 7 July 1947. Seventeen new TPO vehicles were included in the railways' 1947/8 building programme, with what was by then the Western and London Midland Regions having some new stock in operation by February 1948; this new stock replaced both older vehicles and those lost during the war. At this time TPO staff also found that vehicle cleaning was often not to the same standard which prevailed before the war and asked for more disinfectant to be used in toilets 'as a general practice'. Other TPOs were restored during the closing years of the 1940s, but 34 of the prewar total of 77 failed to return. This cutback was caused by the reduced number of deliveries,

mainly responsible for the loss of most of the day mails. A shortage of sorters with an intimate knowledge of apparatus operations was the reason the TPO section published a number of TPO route guides at this time. These showed all the landmarks associated with the use of the apparatus and reminded or informed staff of their locations.

The winter of 1947 was particularly trying for TPO staff, as the following brief extract from *The Traveller* reveals: 'Widespread snow throughout England and Scotland on 5 March 1947, seriously delayed all mails. The Down Special terminated at Carlisle, and the Great West at Plymouth. The Down Special was 559min late at Carlisle; the Great West 564min late at Plymouth. The North West Night Down was 794min late at Carlisle. The Cardiff-Crewe-Cardiff TPOs did not run owing to a blockage between Newport and Hereford. All apparatus working was cancelled. The Up Special was 796min late at Euston, having lost 11hr 30min from Tamworth. This went on for a fortnight, and after the snow there were floods to contend with'. An all-TPOs memo of commendation signed by Chief Superintendent F. G. Fielder and Controller, Circulation & Transport Division, H. G. Dorey was circulated on 20 March.

In 1959 British Rail commenced the construction of a new fleet of TPO rolling stock to replace the pre-Nationalisation vehicles then in use. During the following 18 years 145 vehicles were built, some on secondhand underframes, Nominally there are three types: sorting carriages, stowage vans and brake stowage vans, but the building timespan has meant that there are several variations within each category. The last pre-Nationalisation vehicles were withdrawn by 1978.

On Wednesday 7 August 1963 the Up Special TPO left Aberdeen as usual but by the time it reached London it had hit the headlines in a big way. In the early hours of Thursday morning the train was stopped at false signals between Leighton Buzzard and Cheddington by thieves who then separated the locomotive and the first two coaches from the train. After subduing the loco crew, the front of the train was moved to a convenient underbridge where the coaches were broken into and robbed of the currency they were carrying. Slightly more than £2 million was stolen. The currency was used bank notes being returned to the Bank of England for destruction. The incident became known as the 'Great Train Robbery', and despite the arrest, and subsequent imprisonment, of some of those involved, most of the money was never recovered. It was a black night for both British Rail and the Post Office. In addition to the implementation of various security measures one outcome of the robbery was the ending of the carriage of bullion on TPOs.

In 1968 the Post Office introduced a two-tier postal system. The objective was to reduce the amount of mail posted in the afternoon and requiring next-day delivery. A higher rate was charged for first class mail, for which the customer required a next-day delivery, and a lower rate for second class items which could be sorted at slack times and delivered later. This affected the TPOs as it was decided they should handle only first class items. As the system settled down it became apparent that there was insufficient overnight business to sustain some of the services. The first to go was the Plymouth-Bristol TPO on 3 March 1972. Subsequent service reviews have seen all the short-distance TPOs, and some of the long-distance ones, withdrawn. A number of new TPOs have, however, been introduced, along with modifications to others.

The use of the mail exchange apparatus began to decline after World War 2. This was partly because of the reduction in the number of postal distribution centres with the increased use of motor vehicles for local distribution. Also, the improved acceleration and braking capabilities of diesel and electric locomotives made it possible to introduce new or longer station stops where necessary. Higher speeds also made it increasingly likely that the practice was becoming unsafe. The last apparatus in use was at Penrith, in Cumbria, when the last pickup was made by the Up Special TPO on 1 October 1971 and the last dispatch was made by the North Western Night Down TPO on 3 October 1971.

The Post Office offered to make available sets of apparatus to interested parties who could make use of them. To date, working demonstrations have been established by the Great Western Society at Didcot, using a Great Western Railway vehicle, and by Railway Vehicle Preservations, at Quorn & Woodhouse station on the Great Central Railway, using a London & North Eastern Railway vehicle. There is a possibility that other systems may be installed in the future.

In 1979 the Post Office expanded its overnight airmail service, for first class and Datapost items, with a network based on Speke Airport in Merseyside and also, from 1982, on East Midlands Airport in Leicestershire. The air services are designed to be

Below: **On 10 May 1988** *Mallard* **hauled the 'Pennine Postal' from Manchester Victoria to Scarborough and York. It is seen at Manchester before departure, with TPO stock 80359 and 80389 behind the locomotive.** *Peter Johnson*

complementary to the rail services and they are integrated at some points. By 1995 the air services had become Skynet, a network of 32 chartered flights from 21 airports each night. There are no plans for air to take over from rail, but greater integration of all types of transport will continue to evolve.

The opening of the Liverpool & Manchester Railway in 1830 was commemorated by a set of postage stamps issued on 12 March 1980. The five stamps showed typical L&M rolling stock, one vehicle being a mail coach. On the nights of 11 and 12 March members of the Railway Philatelic Group organised a mass TPO mailing with covers bearing the new stamps. A total of 26 trains were visited, some on both nights. British Rail ran a first day cover train from Manchester to Liverpool and back using *Flying Scotsman*. The real anniversary was celebrated on 11 November 1980, when the Post Office chartered a special train from Liverpool to York hauled by Stanier Pacific *Duchess of Hamilton*, so commemorating 150 years of carrying mail by rail. Similar organised mailings have been arranged for other relevant stamp issues and to record changes to the TPO network.

A new five-year contract between the Post Office and British Rail's Parcels Sector commenced in 1983. It was worth around £40 million a year, paid quarterly in arrears, with penalty payments due for late running and failure to provide accommodation. The contract was divided into two parts: Schedule I, where the Post Office bought space on trains, around 150, including 39 TPOs, and Schedule II, where the Post Office paid a price per bag carried.

The use of temporary TPOs is uncommon but the modernisation of the Crewe station track layout in 1985 and the Birmingham Proof House Junction bridge renewal in 1986 required significant changes to the normal service, including the use of several temporary TPOs. In the former case most of Crewe Station was closed for seven weeks from 3 June. Mail handling therefore transferred to Stafford, with the

Below: **The 'ticket' for the 'Pennine Postal' of 10 May 1988, showing the stamp design as a background.** *Peter Johnson Collection*

TPOs which normally called at Crewe, except for the York-Shrewsbury TPO, calling there instead. To cover the York-Shrewsbury connection a temporary service, the Shrewsbury-Stafford Sorting Carriage, was introduced. The SC was worked to Stafford with the Shrewsbury-York and the Cardiff-Crewe TPOs, the only time that three TPOs have operated in a single train. The return duty, the Stafford-Shrewsbury SC, ran to Shrewsbury with the Crewe-Cardiff TPO.

The Proof House bridge renewal required a major recasting of TPO services for just five nights in February 1986, including temporary Birmingham sections of the Up and Down Specials connecting with the main services at Crewe. A temporary Birmingham section of the North Western Night Down ran between Euston and Birmingham; it returned to London as the Birmingham-London bag tender. A temporary Birmingham section of the Bristol-Derby TPO (and vice versa) left/joined the main train at Worcester, using the permanent datestamps, whilst the Bristol-Derby TPO (and vice versa) used temporary (rubber) datestamps. Temporary bag tenders also operated between Birmingham and Derby and between Birmingham and Longbridge.

On several occasions from 1985 the Post Office invited press and dignitaries to travel on TPOs, as commemorations or to publicise events. The first occasion was on 5 September that year, when the Whitehaven-Huddersfield TPO both carried visitors and was hauled by a steam loco for part of its journey, to publicise the 350th anniversary of the Post Office. During the following five years or so TPOs featured in a number of postal special occasions, usually as demonstrations in chartered passenger trains, where second class mail was used to show sorting on the move.

An interesting revival occurred on 20 January 1986, with the introduction of the Chester Relief Sorting Carriage, a sorting carriage operated by the Head Postmaster of Chester. Carrying postmen from Chester Sorting Office it ran between Chester and Crewe. Whilst at Crewe, for over 3hr, the postmen sorted mail bound for North Wales from the TPOs which called there, the sorting carriage's purpose being to provide improved North Wales deliveries by saving the time previously taken, since the withdrawal of the Crewe-Bangor TPO, by carrying the mail by road to the Chester Sorting Office. The SC actually ran at the same time as the withdrawn Crewe-Bangor service and after the postmen left it at Chester, continued to Bangor as a bag tender, complete with courier to deal with Datapost; the service was withdrawn after 28 May 1994.

The 50th anniversary of the famous *Night Mail* film was marked by the commissioning of a new version, *Night Mail II*, made in the autumn of 1986. This included aerial filming of a train of TPO stock newly painted in Royal Mail red and yellow livery on the Midland main line on 20 September and naming

Class 47 No 47515 *Night Mail* at Derby on 25 September, after which the loco hauled the North Eastern TPO to St Pancras carrying a small press party in a manned buffet car.

Compared to the 1938 TPO centenary celebrations, the 150th anniversary of TPOs on 20 January 1988 was a very low-key affair. Collectors made postings and the author was allowed to travel on the North Western TPO Night Down, the successor of the first TPOs, from Euston to Carlisle.

On 10 May 1988, however, an 18p commemorative postage stamp, one of a set with the theme of 'Transport & Communications', was issued. The main motif of the stamp was the LNER 4-6-2 locomotive No 4468, *Mallard*, for it commemorated the 50th anniversary of that locomotive's record speed run. Of interest to us here, though, is the TPO lineside apparatus tucked in a corner, for the stamp also served to record the 150th anniversary of the TPOs. The day before the stamp was issued, the Post Office chartered a special train called the 'Postal Pullman' which ran from Marylebone to Banbury, hauled by *Mallard* itself. Included in the train were two TPO carriages, Nos 80359/89. They were staffed by 10 postmen from the Great Western TPO, who demonstrated their art by sorting second class mail. For the return journey the train was hauled by Class 47 No 47515 *Night Mail*. The next day the same formation worked another train, this time called the 'Pennine Pullman', from Manchester Victoria to Scarborough and back. The postal demonstration was provided by York-based York-Shrewsbury TPO personnel.

Also in 1988, the Royal Mail and British Rail entered into a new five-year contract. No less than 72 locomotives were dedicated to Post Office letter and parcel traffic and all vehicle maintenance was concentrated at Barton Hill, Bristol, and Cambridge. By now worth £46 million a year, the contract specified service objectives of 90% of its 250 dedicated mail trains, including TPOs, arriving within 10min of right time, after allowances for delays beyond BR's control. Bonuses were to be paid for bettering this, and penalties due for failure. By 1989 85-87% of services were meeting the target; in May 1990 BR received bonuses, £500 for each 1%, for beating the target. It is worth pointing out that the Royal Mail does not seek early arrivals, either, for it then loses sorting time; say six sorters have arrived 10min early, then an hour's sorting has been lost.

An innovation from the late 1980s saw TPOs being displayed at BR depot open days. Most were manned and some offered souvenir covers franked with various datestamps or special postmarks. Usually a sorting carriage was accompanied by a stowage van, but at the Exeter Rail Fair in 1994 a complete Great Western TPO set was provided, along with a Super GUV and a Propelling Control Vehicle. The following list is incomplete but gives some indication of the range covered.

LOCATION	SORTING CARRIAGE NO	DATE
Coalville	80327	1/9/85
Norwich, Crown Point		30/5/87
Coalville		31/5/87
Woking		29/5/88
Coalville	80306	11/6/89
Southend Victoria	80303	8/8/89
Arley (Severn Valley Railway)	80387	13/5/90
Gloucester	80326	1/7/90
Cambridge	80327	29/9/90
York Station (RPG Convention)	80325	20/4/91
Cambridge		14/9/91
Brighton Lovers Walk		22/9/91
Manchester Longsight		25/4/92
Ashford Chart Leacon	80340	6/6/92
Leicester	80327	6/9/92
Wolverton Works	80351	25/9/93
Old Oak Common	80379	19/3/94
Exeter	80385	1/5/94
Worcester	80352	22/5/94
Doncaster	80357	9/7/94
Crewe Basford Hall	80391	21/8/94

From time to time TPO services are subject to review, when services are introduced, modified or withdrawn. For example, in an exercise called 'TPO initiative 91', from 30 September the Peterborough-Crewe TPO was extended to Carlisle, returning via Newcastle and York; the North West Night Down TPO was accelerated and extended to Glasgow. At the same time the Whitehaven-Huddersfield and Huddersfield-Whitehaven TPOs and the Lincoln Sections of the erstwhile Peterborough-Crewe and Crewe-Peterborough TPOs were withdrawn. The benefits were seen to be improvements for customers in the Western Isles, Dumfries, Galloway, Argyll and the Scottish Borders, North Wales, Cheshire, Lancashire and Cumbria who received next-day delivery of letters posted later in the day in East Anglia, London and the Home Counties. The accelerated North Western TPO also provided significant benefits for Scotland from practically the whole of England. The withdrawals were explained, to staff, as follows: 'concentrations and an enhanced transport network have led to a situation where the traffic ... can be given the same level of service by use of other links'. The rolling stock and most of the staff were redeployed to the Peterborough-Carlisle-Peterborough services.

A short-term contract was agreed between the Post Office and British Rail in 1993, to last until 1996. In 1995, when 93% of arrivals were being recorded within 10min of scheduled arrival time, a new contract was agreed, to start in 1996. It promises to breathe new life into the TPO service. To last 10 years, the contract's start will coincide with the introduction to service in 1996 of a major new rail/road interchange facility at Willesden, in north

London. An integral part of the contract is the construction of a fleet of electric multiple units designed to carry containers of mail between Willesden and major provincial centres — more details of this, the Railnet project, are given in Chapter 7.

The preliminary TPO programme for 1996 will see TPOs operating between London and Newcastle, Manchester, Carlisle, Glasgow, Swansea, Plymouth, Crewe and Norwich, together with cross-country services from Newcastle to Bristol and Penzance, Cardiff to Newcastle, Coventry to Glasgow, Dover to Norwich and Peterborough to Carlisle.

The TPOs presently serving London will, from 1996, operate to and from Willesden, the TPO fleet being refurbished to keep it operating at least until the contract expires in 2006. A review of future requirements will take place in 2001, to establish if there will be a continued requirement for TPOs and if there is, to lay down the specification for new rolling stock which will take the TPO service well into the 21st century.

For the time being, however, TPOs are still the best way of moving large volumes of late afternoon/early evening first class post overnight for first delivery the following morning. Their future can be affected, however, by unconsidered events. For example, in 1995 Leicester lost its 29-year connection with TPOs with no notice at all because a new sorting office, called an automated processing centre, had been opened, handily positioned close to the M1/M69 junction but five miles away from the station. As Brian Quinn, Manager TPOs, told the author, talking about network reviews, 'It's all about quality, but if quality can be had by other means then changes will be made'.

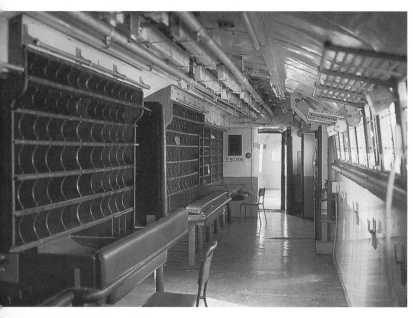

Left: **No 80306 on display at Coalville open day, 11 June 1989.** *Peter Johnson*

Left: **Lord Whitelaw and the Managing Director, Royal Mail Letters, Bill Cockburn, at Carlisle on 6 September 1991. Lord Whitelaw had named sorting carriage No 80320 to publicise the start of the Carlisle-Peterborough TPO the following week.** *Peter Johnson*

2. TPO Services 1838-1995

A list of TPO services follows. It is necessarily abbreviated, being largely restricted to dates of commencement and cessation or alteration. Where the route followed is not obvious from the title this is also given. The early histories have not always been well recorded, which accounts for a certain vagueness regarding some of the older services.

* — TPO operating at time of publication

Aberdeen & Elgin Sorting Carriage
Commenced 24 October 1904. Ceased 3 June 1916. Previously the North of Scotland Sorting Carriage.

Ayr & Carlisle Sorting Tender
Commenced 23 November 1874 and became an SC in 1904. On 1 October 1921 became the Ayr-Carlisle RSC, a title which lasted until 6 November 1929 when it became the Ayr-Carlisle SC. Ceased 9 November 1969.

Bangor Railway Post Office
Ran during the 1850s from Leeds to Holyhead.

Bangor & Crewe Travelling Post Office
This service emerged when the Bangor & Leeds RPO was split into two parts in the 1870s. The datestamps were inscribed 'From East' for the Down working and 'From West' for the Up working. Renamed the Bangor-Crewe TPO on 17 February 1930. Ceased 9 February 1979. A parcel sorting carriage was conveyed between 1885 and 5 November 1915. As with the Bangor RPO, the working was actually to and from Holyhead.

Below: **The Ayr-Carlisle SC at Carrockburn in April 1964.** *Derek Cross*

Bangor & Leeds Railway Post Office
Successor to the Bangor RPO until the creation of the Bangor & Crewe TPO in the 1870s.

Bangor & Normanton Railway Post Office
Possibly the Bangor RPO extended to Normanton to connect with the Midland RPO.

Berwick & Newcastle Sorting Tender
Little is known about this service, although a number of postmark impressions dated 1888 exist.

Birmingham & Crewe Sorting Carriage
The Birmingham & Stafford ST extended, probably from 1885. Became the Birmingham-Crewe SC on 17 February 1930 and the Birmingham-Crewe TPO on 3 November 1930. Ceased 5 March 1967.

Birmingham & Stafford Sorting Tender
Commenced February 1856; replaced by Birmingham & Crewe SC in 1885.

Birmingham-Bristol Travelling Post Office
Founded on 3 July 1938 when the Bristol-Gloucester TPO was extended to Birmingham. Extended to Derby on 27 March 1949.

*Birmingham-Glasgow Travelling Post Office
Commenced 17 May 1993.

Birmingham-Liverpool Railway Post Office
The original experimental TPO which ran in a converted horsebox during 1838.

Birmingham-London Bag Tender
A temporary service which ran between Birmingham and Crewe during the Proof House Junction bridge renewal; the service ran for five nights from 24 February 1986. Late fee mail was, exceptionally, accepted by this bag tender.

Bridlington Sorting Carriage
Serviced by the Hull ST from 5 June 1892, this SC permitted Bridlington's first delivery to commence 35min earlier than formerly. Extended to Leeds from 1913 and ceased on 30 October 1916. Reinstated between Bridlington and Hull only as a summer service from 17 June 1919 to 30 October 1926.

Brighton Sorting Carriage
Commenced 1 July 1859. Extended to Hastings on 1 January 1876. The London terminal was London Bridge.

Brighton & Hastings Sorting Carriage
The Hastings portion of the Brighton SC from 1 January 1876. Ceased 31 March 1916.

Bristol Sorting Carriage
Probably reserved accommodation on the Midland TPO between Derby and Bristol for pre-sorting Bristol mail. Probably ran from the turn of the century until World War 1.

Below: **The Bangor-Crewe TPO at Rhyl on 27 October 1977.** *Larry Goddard*

Bristol & Exeter Railway Post Office
Commenced 1 December 1859. Known as the North Mail, since it connected with the Midland RPO, and to distinguish it from the Day Mail over the same route, which was a connection off a London train. Extended to Newton Abbot in July 1872. Title changed to Bristol & Exeter TPO on an unknown date.

Bristol & Exeter Travelling Post Office (Day Mail)
Commenced 1875. Ceased 1917.

Bristol & Newton Abbot Travelling Post Office
Commenced July 1872. Extended to Plymouth in October 1895.

Bristol & Penzance Travelling Post Office
The Bristol-Plymouth TPO extended to Penzance on 11 February 1896. Cut back to Plymouth because of the war on 14 August 1916 and renamed accordingly on 14 April 1930.

Bristol-Birmingham Travelling Post Office
See the entry for the Birmingham-Bristol TPO.

Bristol-Derby Travelling Post Office
Commenced on 27 March 1949 when the Birmingham-Bristol TPO was extended to Derby. Replaced by Derby-Penzance TPO from 3 October 1988.

Bristol-Derby Travelling Post Office Derby Section
For the five nights of 24-28 February 1986 the Bristol-Derby TPO was operated in two sections due to the renewal by British Rail of Proof House bridge at Birmingham. The main service terminated at Birmingham, whilst a temporary service also operated from Derby through to Bristol but avoiding Birmingham.

Bristol-Gloucester Travelling Post Office
Commenced 1 June 1910 as the Gloucester & Bristol

TPO. A bag tender had been operated on this route from 1899. Extended to Birmingham on 3 July 1938.

Bristol-London Sorting Carriage
Commenced in the 1860s. Renamed the Bristol-London TPO on 7 July 1930. The Up was not reinstated after World War 1 until 1932. Ceased 21 September 1940.

*Bristol-Penzance Travelling Post Office
The truncated Derby-Penzance TPO, commenced 31 May 1994.

Bristol-Plymouth Travelling Post Office
Created by extending the Bristol & Newton Abbot TPO to Plymouth in October 1895. Extended to Penzance on 11 February 1896. Cut back to Plymouth in 1916, reverting to the Bristol-Plymouth title on 14 April 1930. Ceased on 3 March 1972.

Bristol, Shrewsbury & Normanton Travelling Post Office
Created on 15 October 1895 when the Shrewsbury & Normanton TPO was extended to Bristol. Extended to York on 1 July 1902 becoming the Bristol, Shrewsbury & York TPO.

Bristol, Shrewsbury & York Travelling Post Office
Commenced 1 July 1902 as described above. Became the Cardiff-York TPO in June 1910.

Caledonian Railway Post Office
A Night Mail commenced operating between Carlisle and Glasgow 10 March 1848. Later that year extended to Perth, avoiding Glasgow. A Day Mail started in 1848 was extended to Aberdeen in 1849, the Night Mail following suit in 1850, although it was 1871 before sorting was carried out after Perth. On 1 February 1859 the Night Down became a Limited Mail, ie the Post Office permitted a limited amount of

passenger accommodation to be included in the train formation. From January 1870 the services became the Caledonian TPO, with distinguishing datestamps for the day and night operations. An exclusive 'special' mail between Euston and Aberdeen was introduced on 1 July 1885; four passenger coaches were permitted from Perth. The stock used on the Up Limited and the Up Special was returned North on the Night Down, which became known as the Down Special. The Night Up ceased in 1917 and its business transferred to the Up Special which became the Up Special TPO. On 1 September 1923 the Night Down amalgamated with the North Western Night Down to become the Down Special TPO. After a number of minor revisions the Day Mails were terminated at Perth and Carlisle in 1924. An Edinburgh portion started to serve the Day Up, also in 1924. A Glasgow portion followed in 1935. Both were attached to the main train at Carstairs. Withdrawn 30 September 1988.

Cambridge District Sorting Carriage
Started as a sorting tender in 1850, the DSC superseding it in 1863. Ceased in 1869. Mails from London suburbs were collected on the Down run for sorting on Up trains.

Cardiff & York Travelling Post Office
In June 1910 the Bristol, Shrewsbury and York TPO was extended to Cardiff. On 4 October 1920 the working was divided to give the Cardiff-Crewe RSC and the Shrewsbury-York RSC.

*Cardiff-Crewe Railway Sorting Carriage
Created when the Cardiff-York TPO operation was split into two on 4 October 1920. Became a SC in 1929 and a TPO on 14 April 1930. Amalgamated with Shrewsbury-York TPO to create Cardiff-York TPO from 16 May 1988. Re-established as Cardiff-Crewe TPO from 31 May 1994.

Cardiff-York Travelling Post Office
Established by combining the Cardiff-Crewe TPO with the Shrewsbury-York TPO from 16 May 1988. The service stopped additionally at Manchester Piccadilly. Finished 27 May 1994 and replaced by new Cardiff-Crewe TPO.

Carlisle & Ayr Sorting Tender
Commenced 23 November 1874 and became an SC in 1904. On 1 October 1921 became the Carlisle-Ayr RSC, a title which lasted until 6 November 1929 when it became the Carlisle-Ayr SC. Ceased 9 November 1969.

Carlisle & Edinburgh Sorting Tender
Commenced experimentally in September 1858 and made permanent in 1860. Withdrawn between 1 December 1877 and May 1885 when the duty was

Left: **With 'Princess Coronation' 4-6-2 No 46228** *Duchess of Rutland* **at the head, the Crewe-Bangor TPO waits to leave Crewe on 7 March 1964.**
John Clarke

		SCHEDULED TIMES MON-FRI	ACTUAL TIME	THE CAUSE OF DELAY SHOULD BE FULLY STATED AFTER CONSULTING THE GUARD OR OTHER RAILWAY OFFICIALS. (TPO ORDER 322/85 REFERS)
STATIONS				
BERTHED PLATFORM				
CREWE	DEP	00.49		
DERBY	ARR	01.55		
	DEP	02.10		
NOTTINGHAM	ARR	02.30		
	DEP	02.40		
GRANTHAM	ARR	03.11		
	DEP	03.17		
PETERBOROUGH	ARR	03.53		

10/85   CREWE - PETERBOROUGH TPO   TPO 705   DATE STAMP

_____ day

NOS OF CARRIAGES
OR STOWAGE VANS   SEARCHED BY
PE POT
PE POS
LATE POSTINGS
TPO WATCH

DATE STAMPS KEYS RECORDS FIRST AID OUTFIT WINDING HANDLE AND ALL STORES SHOWN ON THE STANDARD LIST INTACT.
AT DEPARTURE _____
AT TERMINAL _____

CODING TOOL   RECEIVED BY   RETURNED TO

REPORTING PARTICULARS

A	ARR DERBY ARR PETERBOROUGH	B	C
D		E	F

Right: **Timebill for the Crewe-Peterborough TPO, 30 September 1985.**
Peter Johnson Collection

replaced by a Carstairs-Edinburgh working. In January 1922 the Up working became the Edinburgh Section of the Up Special. The Down became the Carlisle-Edinburgh SC in October 1924 and the Carlisle-Edinburgh TPO from 3 October 1988.

Carlisle-Edinburgh Travelling Post Office
Established 3 October 1988, replacing the Up Special TPO Edinburgh Section. Last run on 14 May 1993.

*Carlisle-Peterborough Travelling Post Office
Crewe-Peterborough TPO operated to Carlisle and routed instead via Newcastle and York, commenced 30 September 1991. Inaugurated on 6 September 1991, when sorting carriage 80320 was named *The Borders Mail* at Carlisle by Lord Whitelaw, the Newcastle-based carriage being allocated to the service when first operated.

Carmarthen & Newcastle Emlyn Sorting Carriage
The Llandyssul Sorting Tender, a Carmarthen-Llandyssul duty, extended to Newcastle Emlyn in July 1895. Ceased 1 May 1904.

Carnforth & Whitehaven Travelling Post Office
The Whitehaven ST, introduced in 1875, used a datestamp with this title between 1891 and 1911; its duties don't appear to have changed as a result,

although the service was designated a sorting carriage in 1904.

Chester & Crewe Parcel Travelling Post Office
Commenced July 1885 attached to the Bangor-Crewe TPO; extended to Bangor September 1885.

Chester & Holyhead Railway Post Office
Commenced 1854; extended to London (Euston) 1860.

Chester Relief Sorting Tender
Commenced 20 January 1986, a Chester-Crewe-Chester working which operated in the same times as the former Crewe-Bangor TPO. Most sorting was carried out whilst the vehicle was static at Crewe to save mail addressed to North Wales and coming off the TPOs there having to be taken into Chester Sorting Office. The late fee posting facility, which was advertised when the service was introduced, was quickly withdrawn. The service was controlled by the Head Postmaster at Chester and was withdrawn after operation on 27 May 1994.

Continental Night Mail
Commenced 1 September 1867, between Dover and London (Cannon Street). A Down service was introduced in 1879. Ceased 1915 but reintroduced as the London-Dover RSC in 1922.

Cornwall Sorting Tender

Commencement probably followed shortly after the Cornwall Railway opened its line from Plymouth to Truro in 1859. The duty connected with the London & Exeter TPO, the night mail, and the Bristol & Exeter, the north mail. The former ceased in 1895, on the creation of the Great Western TPO, and the latter in 1896 on the creation of the Bristol & Penzance TPO.

Crewe & Manchester Sorting Carriage

The Manchester Sorting Tender apparently renamed in 1908. Redesignated the Crewe-Manchester RSC from October 1915. An additional Down working was established at the same time. Ceased 23 September 1939.

Crewe-Bangor Travelling Post Office

See the entry for the Bangor & Crewe TPO.

Crewe-Birmingham Sorting Carriage

See the entry for the Birmingham & Crewe SC.

Crewe-Cardiff Railway Sorting Carriage

See the entry for the Cardiff-Crewe RSC.

*Crewe-Cardiff Travelling Post Office

See the entry for the Cardiff-Crewe RSC.

Crewe-Glasgow Sorting Carriage

Finished on 14 May 1993.

Crewe-Liverpool Sorting Carriage

Commenced 1 July 1885. Ceased 23 September 1939.

Crewe-Peterborough Travelling Post Office

Commenced 6 June 1966 with a Lincoln Section which ran to and from Crewe, joining/leaving the main train at Derby. Crewe-Peterborough working diverted via Grantham from 30 September 1985, the Up North Eastern TPO making a compensatory stop at Leicester. Last night 27 September 1971, when replaced by Carlisle-Peterborough TPO, operating via Newcastle and York, from 30 September 1991.

Dartmoor Railway Sorting Tender

Little is known of this service which may have operated in conjunction with Army manoeuvres in 1873.

Derby & St Pancras Sorting Tender

Commenced 1877. Renamed the London & Derby SC on 13 July 1908.

Derby-Bristol Travelling Post Office

See the entry for the Bristol-Derby TPO.

Derby-Bristol Travelling Post Office Derby Section

See the entry for the Bristol-Derby TPO Derby Section.

Derby-London Travelling Post Office

Created 3 October 1988. Conveyed with the Midland TPO from Newcastle to Derby. Last run on 26 May 1995.

Derby-Penzance Travelling Post Office

Created by combining the Derby-Bristol TPO with the Great Western TPO's Bristol-Penzance duties from 3 October 1988. Last run on 27 May 1994, and replaced by the Bristol-Penzance TPO from 31 May 1994.

Dingwall-Perth Railway Sorting Carriage

Created when a number of changes were made to the workings of the Highland SC in November 1917. The Up trip had been the Day Mail, the Down the Night. Extended to Helmsdale 6 August 1923.

Doncaster-London Travelling Post Office

The truncated Leeds-London TPO, created 7 March 1932. Ceased 21 September 1940.

Dover-London Railway Sorting Carriage

The Continental Night Mail renamed when reintroduced 4 September 1922. The London terminal was Holborn Viaduct except on Sundays when it was Victoria. Ceased 5 October 1923.

*Dover-Manchester Travelling Post Office

Operated from 16 May 1988. Routed via Reading, Coventry, Birmingham and Crewe. Launched by means of a special passenger train which ran between Dover and Reading on 11 May 1986; the train of mainly Pullman coaches included two sorting carriages, Nos 80359/89. Sorting was demonstrated by postmen recruited to work the new service; an inspector had previously worked on the South Eastern TPO.

Down Special Travelling Post Office

Created on 1 September 1923 by the amalgamation of the Night North Western and Caledonian TPOs, giving a through working from Euston to Aberdeen. Ceased 14 May 1993.

Down Special Travelling Post Office Birmingham Section

A temporary service which ran between Birmingham and Crewe during the Proof House Junction bridge renewal; the service ran for five nights from 24 February 1986.

*East Anglian Travelling Post Office

Created when the Norwich ST, which ran from Liverpool Street via Cambridge and Ely, was modified to run via Ipswich on 3 March 1929. The King's Lynn Section ran from Haughley Junction; on 30 October 1949 it was extended to Peterborough and Ipswich was the junction for the Peterborough portion from

1966. The Peterborough Section finished on 11 May 1990.

Edinburgh & Berwick Sorting Tender
Little is known of this service which probably ran in conjunction with the Edinburgh & Newcastle ST in the latter half of the 19th century.

Edinburgh & Carlisle Sorting Tender
See the entry for the Carlisle & Edinburgh ST.

Edinburgh & Carstairs Sorting Tender
Commenced 1 December 1877. Down working ceased 1 July 1885. Up working ceased before World War 1.

Edinburgh & Glasgow Sorting Tender
Operated for a brief period *circa* 1870.

Edinburgh & Newcastle Sorting Tender
Day and Night Mails commenced in the 1870s. The duties of the Day Mail were absorbed by the North Eastern Day TPO when that working was extended to Edinburgh on 30 September 1908. The Up Night ceased on 22 May 1916. The establishment of the London-York-Edinburgh RSC coincided with the cessation of the Down Night duty.

Edinburgh-Carlisle Travelling Post Office
See the entry for the Carlisle-Edinburgh TPO.

Edinburgh-York Sorting Carriage
The Up North Eastern TPO Day Mail was reduced to operating between Edinburgh and York on 17 October 1917. The duty was named the Edinburgh-York SC on 18 January 1926. It became a TPO on 14 April 1930. Withdrawn after 27 September 1985.

Exeter & Torrington Sorting Carriage
Commenced 12 August 1906. Ceased 5 May 1917.

Fife Sorting Tender
Commenced operating between Burntisland and Tayport 1884. Extended to Dundee in 1887 and Edinburgh in 1890. The Day Mail ceased on 6 November 1915, the Night Mail following on 14 October 1917.

Galloway Sorting Tender
Commenced operating between Dumfries and Stranraer on 1 May 1871. Extended to Carlisle 1 July 1885. Designated a TPO on 14 July 1930 and ceased 1940.

Glasgow Sorting Tender
Operating between Glasgow and Carlisle, this service commenced experimentally in September 1858 and was made permanent in March 1860. Known as the Glasgow & Carlisle SC from *circa* 1904.

Glasgow & Carlisle Sorting Carriage
As the Glasgow ST. Extended to Preston in 1914 and named the Glasgow-Preston RSC. Up services operated with the Up Special and the Up Limited until 1 February 1917 when these services amalgamated. Two Down services restricted to Glasgow and Carlisle operated as the Carlisle-Glasgow RSC until February 1922 when they amalgamated and were extended to Preston, becoming the Preston-Glasgow RSC.

*Glasgow-Birmingham Travelling Post Office
See the entry for the Birmingham-Glasgow Travelling Post Office.

Glasgow-Preston Railway Sorting Carriage
As the Glasgow & Carlisle SC. Extended to Crewe on 15 December 1926 becoming the Crewe-Glasgow RSC, working with the Down Special from Crewe to Carstairs. Designated a sorting carriage from 6 November 1929.

Gloucester & Bristol TPO
Commenced 1 June 1910. Extended to Birmingham 3 July 1938.

Below: **A commemorative timebill for the last night of the Edinburgh-York TPO.** *Peter Johnson Collection*

EDINBURGH - YORK TPO

FINAL JOURNEY
FRIDAY 27th SEPTEMBER 1985

COMMEMORATIVE TIME SHEET

EDINBURGH		
Berwick-Upon-Tweed	dep	2035
	arr	2122
Alnmouth	dep	2126
	arr	2155
Morpeth	dep	2158
	arr	2215
Newcastle-Upon-Tyne	dep	2217
	arr	2238
Durham	dep	2305
	arr	2320
Darlington	dep	2324
	arr	2342
YORK	dep	2348
	arr	0027

59 YEARS OF SERVICE
Edinburgh-York SC   1926 - 1930
Edinburgh-York TPO   1930 - 1985

Gloucester & Tamworth Railway Post Office

Commenced 1 November 1850. Became part of the Midland RPO, which operated between Gloucester and Newcastle, before 1855. Replaced by the London-Leeds RSC 10 July 1922.

Grand Northern Railway Post Office

On 10 November 1838 this name was applied to the London & Birmingham Railway Post Office, which had been running to Warrington since 1 October 1838 and Preston from 7 November, the latter service extension coinciding with the opening of the North Union Railway. On 10 November two handstamps inscribed 'Missent to the G.N.R. Post Office' were issued to the Mail Coach Office, replacing an earlier one inscribed 'Missent to London & Birmingham Railway Office'. Lancaster was served from June 1840. Reverted to a Preston terminal February 1841 but extended to Lancaster again on 15 August 1844. Became the North Western RPO in 1847.

Great Northern Sorting Tender

This was a Day Mail which started operating between King's Cross and York on 1 March 1875. Became a sorting carriage in 1902.

Great Northern Travelling Post Office (Midday Mail)

A King's Cross-Doncaster working which commenced on 1 May 1885. Extended to York 28 February 1903. In 1910 it left King's Cross at 1.30pm (!) and arrived at Doncaster in 2hr 54min, considered a fast timing for 156 miles; thereafter the TPO was taken on to York by a local train. Ceased 6 November 1915.

Great Northern Travelling Post Office

Commenced 24 January 1910 between King's Cross and Newcastle. Amalgamated with the Newcastle & Edinburgh SC to form the London-York-Edinburgh RSC on 10 July 1922.

Great Western District Sorting Tender

Commenced as a replacement for the Great Western Sunday ST, November 1859, operating between Paddington and Exeter. Ceased 1869.

Great Western Sunday Sorting Tender

Commenced operating between Paddington and Swindon 12 April 1850. Replaced by the Great Western DST 1859.

*Great Western Travelling Post Office

Created by the amalgamation of the London & Exeter RPO and the Cornwall ST in 1896. Extended to Penzance 1 January 1902. The Up arrival at Paddington made a connection with the 5.10am TPO from Liverpool Street; if it was late a cab was hired to carry the bags — it is recorded in 1899 that on one occasion the cabman refused, perhaps he didn't rate

the GPO as a tipper, only to later find himself barred from picking up fares from Paddington station! Such a problem did not arise after the opening of the Post Office Railway. On one night in October 1959 a restaurant car was attached to the Down to carry 42 journalists to publicise the introduction of the BR TPO stock.

Diverted from Bristol and cut back to Plymouth on 3 October 1988, when Bristol-Penzance duties were taken on by the Derby-Penzance TPO.

Greenock Sorting Tender

Commenced March 1866, operating between Glasgow and Greenock. Ceased late 1870s.

Grimsby & Lincoln Sorting Carriage

Commenced 1850s. Ceased 8 November 1915.

Grimsby & Peterborough Sorting Carriage

Commenced 1 April 1900. Ceased 30 March 1917.

Halifax Sorting Tender

Operated for a short time after 1871.

Hastings & Brighton Sorting Carriage

See the entry for the Brighton & Hastings SC.

Helmsdale-Dingwall Railway Sorting Carriage

Commenced 6 August 1923. Became the Highland TPO (Northern Section) from 2 July 1930.

Highland Sorting Carriage

Commenced between Inverness and Aviemore June 1864. Extended to Perth July 1870. By 1876 the Night Mail had been extended to Bonar Bridge and the Day Mail to Novar. In 1876 the Night Mail was extended to Golspie and the Day Mail to Bonar Bridge. The Night Mail was extended again, to Helmsdale, in the 1880s and the Day Mail was restricted to operating between Inverness and Bonar Bridge. A number of changes took place in 1917, resulting in the Night Up and Day Down services ceasing. The Day Up and the Night Down became known as the Dingwall-Perth RSC.

Highland Travelling Post Office

In July 1930 the Perth-Helmsdale RSC and the Helmsdale-Dingwall RSC became the Highland TPO (Southern Section) and the Highland TPO (Northern Section) respectively. The Northern Section was withdrawn after 4 November 1967 and the Southern Section became simply the Highland TPO. Withdrawn 7 October 1978.

Holyhead-London Travelling Post Office

Day and Night Mails commenced on 1 October 1860. The Day Mail ceased on 30 September 1939, the Night on 31 August 1940. This was the famous Irish Mail.

Right: **Stock (Nos 80439, 80327, 80325) for the Derby-Bristol TPO being shunted on to the passenger portion at Derby on 17 May 1985.** *C. J. Tuffs*

Below: **A TPO working on the Great Northern Railway, possibly at Hadley Wood.** *Collection Brian White*

Bottom: **The Great Western TPO (Up) east of Par in July 1955.** *R. C. Riley*

Huddersfield-Whitehaven Travelling Post Office

The Whitehaven-Stalybridge TPO extended to Huddersfield on 2 January 1966. Last night 27 September 1991.

Hull Sorting Tender

Commenced 2 December 1867 between Hull and Milford Junction. Extended to Normanton 22 April 1869. Extended to Leeds 1903. Designated an SC from 1904. Became the Hull-Leeds SC from 29 September 1914. Ceased 30 September 1917.

Ipswich District Sorting Carriage

Commenced 14 July 1858 between Ipswich and Shoreditch. Ceased 1869.

Ipswich Sorting Tender

Commenced 1872. Became the London-Ipswich TPO on 3 March 1929.

Ipswich Sunday Sorting Tender

Commenced 20 April 1850. Absorbed by the Ipswich DSC.

Ipswich-London Travelling Post Office

The Ipswich ST renamed from 3 March 1929. Extended to Norwich on 3 May 1931.

Leeds-Hull Sorting Carriage

See the entry for the Hull ST.

Leeds & London Sorting Tender

On 4 March 1901 the London & Doncaster ST was extended to Leeds and renamed. The Down duty ceased from 6 November 1915. The Up became the Leeds-London RSC Up on 10 July 1922. (The Great Northern SC became the Down at the same time.) Designated a TPO on 17 February 1930. Reverted to being a Doncaster-London working and named accordingly from 7 March 1932.

Lincoln-Tamworth Sorting Carriage

Known as the Lincoln ST, this service commenced on 20 May 1867. It was entitled the Lincoln-Tamworth SC from 30 September 1919. Ceased 21 September 1940.

Lincoln Sorting Tender

See the entry for the Lincoln-Tamworth SC.

Below: **A parcels train hauled by 'Western' class D1073** *Western Bulwark* **passes Great Western TPO stock berthed between Ponsandane and Marazion on 9 April 1973.** *J. R. Besley*

Below right: **The Holyhead-London TPO (Day) (or the Up Irish Mail) passing Shilton. The LNWR sorting carriage is second from the locomotive, 'King George V' class 4-4-0 No 2370** *Dovedale.* *Real Photos*

Liverpool & Huddersfield Railway Sorting Carriage
Commenced 1 July 1899. Became a TPO from 14 April 1930. Ceased 1 January 1965.

Liverpool & London Travelling Post Office
Commenced 1860s. Ceased 1918.

Llandyssul Sorting Tender
This service commenced between Llandyssul and Carmarthen on 14 December 1875. There was a Night Mail in each direction and a day mail to Llandyssul which returned empty. Extended to Newcastle Emlyn in July 1895. Withdrawn 1 May 1904.

London & Birmingham Railway Post Office
Commenced 22 May 1838, between Euston and Denbigh Hall, where the London & Birmingham Railway then terminated, as the London & Birmingham RPO. Extended to Preston on 7 November 1838 and renamed the Grand Northern Railway Post Office on 10 November that year. A Day Mail had been introduced early in 1839. On 23 November 1839 the *Literary World* reported 'The speed of the mail trains ... is as follows: the day mail leaves the Euston Grove Station at half-past nine in the morning, and arrives at Birmingham in five hours. A stoppage of eight minutes is allowed at Tring, ten minutes at Wolverton, three minutes at Weedon, and nine minutes at Coventry; making a total of twenty-five minutes occupied for stoppages, and only four hours, thirty-five minutes in performing the journey of 112 miles 4 furlongs. The night mail leaves Euston Square at half-past eight, and completes the distance in five hours and a half.' The illustration which accompanied the article has 'Grand Northern Railway Post Office' inscribed on the carriage door.

London & Brighton Sorting Carriage
Commenced 1 July 1859. Extended to become the London & Hastings SC from 1 January 1876. A London & Brighton Day Mail was established in the 1880s. From 1 December 1895 the Hastings service was reorganised, being divided into the London & Brighton SC and the Brighton & Hastings SC, these being Night Mails. The Down Night and Up Day Brighton duties ceased 5 March 1910. The Up Night and Down Day followed on 31 March 1916.

London-Bristol Sorting Carriage
See the entry for the Bristol-London SC.

London & Crewe Sorting Carriage
The London & Stafford SC extended to Crewe from 1 May 1876. Ceased 30 March 1918.

London & Derby Sorting Carriage
Commenced 13 July 1908 when the Derby & St Pancras ST was renamed. Ceased 27 September 1918.

London & Doncaster Sorting Tender
Commenced 1 March 1891. Extended to Leeds on 4 March 1901.

London & Dover Sorting Carriage (Continental Night Mail)
See the entry for the Continental Night Mail.

London & Dover Sorting Carriage (French Day Mail)
Commenced 30 April 1860. Ceased during World War 1.

London & Dover Sorting Carriage (Ostend Day Mail)
Commenced 1 August 1862. Date of withdrawal not known.

London-Dover Railway Sorting Carriage
The Continental Night Mail resumed on 4 September 1922 with this title. Ceased 5 October 1923 and replaced by the London & Newhaven RSC.

London & Exeter Railway Post Office
Commenced 1 February 1855. Amalgamated with the Cornwall ST to become the Great Western TPO on 26 November 1895.

London & Folkestone Sorting Carriage
The rerouted and renamed London & Queenborough SC after 1 May 1911. Ceased 1915.

London-Holyhead Travelling Post Office
See the entry for the Holyhead-London TPO.

London-Holyhead Travelling Post Office (Canadian Mail)
Commenced 1 September 1895. Ceased before 1908.

London-Holyhead Travelling Post Office (USA Mail)
Commenced 6 April 1895. Ceased November 1914.

London-Ipswich Travelling Post Office
See the entry for the Ipswich-London TPO.

London & Leeds Railway Sorting Carriage
See the entry for the Leeds & London RSC.

London-Newhaven Railway Sorting Carriage
Created when the Southern Railway decided to concentrate its Continental services on Newhaven, 7 October 1923. Became an SC in July 1929. Ceased 4 September 1939.

London-Norwich Travelling Post Office
Created on 3 May 1931 when the Ipswich-London TPO was extended to Norwich. The Down Mail ceased on 9 September 1939 for the war, and was replaced by a bag tender in 1948. Both services withdrawn on 11 May 1990.

London & Queenborough Sorting Tender
Commenced January 1891. Ceased 1 May 1911 when the service was diverted to Folkestone.

London-Shrewsbury Travelling Post Office
Commenced 16 May 1988. Part of the North Western TPO Night Down to Rugby, then via Coventry and Birmingham. In the reverse direction connected to the Up Special TPO at Rugby. Ceased on 14 May 1993.

London-York-Edinburgh Railway Sorting Carriage
Created 10 July 1922 by combining the Great Northern TPO with the Newcastle & Edinburgh SC. Designated a TPO on 17 February 1930. Withdrawn after 27 September 1985.

Manchester Sorting Tender
Commenced 14 March 1864 between Manchester and Crewe. Renamed Manchester & Crewe SC *circa* 1908. Became the Manchester-Crewe RSC from October 1915. Two services operated from Crewe to Manchester from this time. Withdrawn for the war, 29 October 1916. The service was reintroduced by 1922 when it was known as the Manchester-Crewe SC. Ceased 23 September 1939.

*Manchester-Dover Travelling Post Office
See the entry for the Dover-Manchester TPO.

Manchester-Glasgow Sorting Carriage
Commenced 10 September 1951. Ceased 3 June 1977.

Midland District Sorting Tender
Commenced, between Euston and Normanton, via Rugby, Leicester and Derby, 22 February 1859. Ceased 14 June 1869. The Up service was via the GN route.

Midland Railway Post Office Day
Commenced, between Rugby and Newcastle, 1 June 1862 when the Leeds & Rugby RPO and the York & Newcastle RPO combined. Ceased February 1873 when the York & Newcastle was reinstated.

Above right: **On 16 January 1987 the Midland and Derby-Bristol TPOs ran through Worcester Shrub Hill for the last time, an unofficial headboard drawing attention to the event on the former.**
Stephen Widdowson

Right: **Entitled 'A night time scene on Platform 10 King's Cross Station' by the photographer, on the left is LNER sorting carriage No 70301, originally No 2152, built in 1933 at York. The working is probably the London-York-Edinburgh TPO.** *C. R. L. Coles*

IV97
MIDLAND TPO
last run through
WORCESTER

Above: **No 86401 in charge of the Manchester-Dover TPO at Crewe on 17 May 1995.** *Peter Johnson*

Centre left: **Sorting on the North Eastern TPO (Up) between Derby and St Pancras on the morning of 27 September 1986. In the foreground an address is being checked with a colleague.** *Peter Johnson*

Lower left: **Bags being unloaded from the North Eastern TPO (Up) at Bedford on the morning of 27 September 1986.** *Peter Johnson*

*Midland Travelling Post Office

Commenced 1855 by the union of the Gloucester & Tamworth and the Rugby & Newcastle Night Mail services, extended to Bristol at the same time. Until 1990 the datestamps of this service showed the Up and Down duties respectively as 'going south' and 'going north', the word 'going' often being abbreviated 'G.G.'. Reduced to a Bristol-Derby (and vice versa) service, but with one vehicle going on to, and from, Newcastle on the North Eastern TPO from, and to, Derby, from 30 September 1985. Reverted to a full Bristol-Newcastle (and vice versa) service from 3 October 1988, but conveying the Derby-London TPO from Newcastle to Derby and the Yorkshire TPO from Derby to Newcastle. From 1990 the Yorkshire TPO ran independently throughout.

Newcastle-on-Tyne Sorting Tender

Commenced March 1876 between York and Newcastle but later extended to Normanton. Operated in conjunction with the Midland TPO. Ceased during World War 1.

Newcastle-London Railway Sorting Carriage

The Great Northern TPO duty after the creation of the London-York-Edinburgh TPO on 10 July 1922. Renamed the North Eastern TPO Night Up on 18 January 1926.

Newhaven-London Railway Sorting Carriage

See the entry for the London-Newhaven RSC.

Normanton & Stalybridge Travelling Post Office

Created when the Leeds & Bangor RPO was divided into two in the 1870s. Combined with the Shrewsbury & Crewe ST 31 January 1893.

*North East Travelling Post Office

The renamed North Eastern TPO strengthened to take traffic from the then recently withdrawn Yorkshire and Derby-London TPOs. Commenced 30 May 1995.

North Eastern Travelling Post Office (Day Mail)

Created 2 July 1895 when the York & Newcastle TPO was extended to Normanton and renamed. Absorbed the Edinburgh & Newcastle SC, another Day Mail, on 1 October 1908. The Down duty ceased 29 July 1916 and the Up ceased to run south of York after 17 October 1921. It became the Edinburgh-York SC from 18 January 1926.

North Eastern Travelling Post Office (Night Down)

Commenced 18 January 1926 between King's Cross and Edinburgh. York-Edinburgh section terminated and the service was diverted to operate from St Pancras via Derby, where it connected with the Midland TPO, on 30 September 1985. Reverted to King's Cross from 3 October 1988. Became the North East TPO Down from 30 May 1995.

North Eastern Travelling Post Office (Night Up)

From 18 January 1926 the Newcastle-London RSC was renamed thus. Diverted to St Pancras via Derby, to where it conveyed one vehicle for the Midland TPO, on 30 September 1985. Reverted to King's Cross from 3 October 1988. On 25 September 1986 this TPO was used for the making of the film *Night Mail II* between Derby and London. A buffet car was attached to the train and carried a small press party. Became the North East TPO Up from 30 May 1995.

North of Scotland Sorting Carriage

Commenced 1 January 1886 replacing an unnamed service which had been operating between Aberdeen and Keith. Extended to Elgin in May 1886 but cut back to Buckie in July 1889. Became the Aberdeen & Elgin SC on 21 November 1904 although it had been operating to Elgin since 1899.

*North West Travelling Post Office Down

First ran, operating between London and Carlisle, on 17 May 1993.

*North West Travelling Post Office Up

First ran, operating out of the Glasgow-Birmingham TPO from Crewe, on 17 May 1993.

North Western District Sorting Carriage

Commenced between Euston and Crewe 5 May 1857. Extended to Preston 31 January 1859. Ceased 21 July 1869.

North Western Sunday Sorting Tender

Operated between Euston and Crewe in the 1850s/60s.

North Western Travelling Post Office (Day Mail)

The Grand Northern RPO renamed in 1847 when operating between Euston and Perth. By 1859 it was running only to Carlisle and by 1881 the Up trip was terminating at Wigan, although it was extended to Crewe during that year. By 1915 the Up duty had been diverted to Liverpool. Ceased before 1922.

North Western Travelling Post Office (Midday Mail)

Commenced between Euston and Crewe 1 March 1883. Ceased 6 November 1915.

North Western Travelling Post Office (10pm Mail)

Commenced 1 July 1885 between Euston and Carlisle. From 12 July 1926 it was renamed the North Western TPO Night Down. Always known by its staff as the 'ten o'clock' although for many years it left Euston an hour later. An account of a visit to this TPO in 1889 recorded that it consisted of nine vehicles, a Guard's brake van, for the Railway Company's parcels; Edinburgh letter and parcel carriage; Aberdeen parcel carriage; Aberdeen letter carriage, with apparatus working between Carlisle and Aberdeen undertaken;

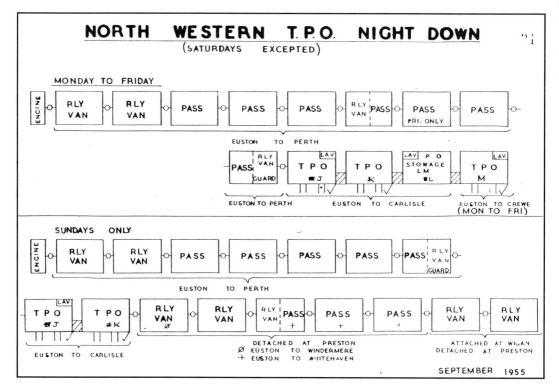

NORTH WESTERN T.P.O. NIGHT DOWN
(SATURDAYS EXCEPTED)

MONDAY TO FRIDAY

ENGINE — RLY VAN — RLY VAN — PASS — PASS — PASS — RLY VAN / PASS — PASS (FRI. ONLY) — PASS

EUSTON TO PERTH

PASS — RLY VAN / GUARD — T P O / ☎ J — T P O / k — LAV / P O STOWAGE LM / ☎L — T P O / M

EUSTON TO PERTH — EUSTON TO CARLISLE — EUSTON TO CREWE (MON TO FRI)

SUNDAYS ONLY

ENGINE — RLY VAN — RLY VAN — PASS — PASS — PASS — PASS — PASS / RLY VAN GUARD

EUSTON TO PERTH

T P O / ☎ J — T P O / ☎ K — RLY VAN / ∅ — RLY VAN — RLY VAN / + PASS — PASS / + — PASS / ⊣ — RLY VAN — RLY VAN

EUSTON TO CARLISLE

∅ DETACHED AT PRESTON / EUSTON TO WINDERMERE
+ EUSTON TO WHITEHAVEN

ATTACHED AT WIGAN / DETACHED AT PRESTON

SEPTEMBER 1955

Glasgow letters, with apparatus working between Euston and Carlisle undertaken; Glasgow letters; Glasgow parcels; a second Guard's brake, for Railway Company's parcels; stowage van for Company's parcels and Post Office bags and baskets.

Sometime before 1937 the TPO received a visit from TRH the Duke and Duchess of York, later King George VI and Queen Elizabeth. The Royal party was *en route* to the Royal train at Euston and, noticing the men working on the TPO, stopped to see what was going on. They toured the train, spoke to all the men and received a demonstration of the apparatus. Upon their departure the Duke and Duchess shook hands with the officer in charge, Teddy Pass, who for weeks afterwards wore a glove on his hand, but refused to take the advice of an irreverent young member of the team who enquired 'Why don't you pickle it in vinegar, guv'nor?'

From 16 May 1988 the train included the London-Shrewsbury TPO as far as Rugby. Became the North West TPO Down from 17 May 1993.

North Western Travelling Post Office (Night Down)
Commenced 8 May 1847 between Euston and Carlisle. North of Carlisle it ran with the Caledonian RPO. In 1905 this TPO was recorded as consisting of 10 vehicles: two brakes and eight postal, and having a crew of 30, whose salaries ranged from £68 to £160 before payment of trip allowance. After 31 August 1923 became part of the Down Special when it was amalgamated with

the Caledonian TPO (Night Mail). From 12 July 1926 the name was given to the 10pm Mail.

North Western Travelling Post Office (Night Up)
Commenced 8 May 1847 between Carlisle and Euston. The Caledonian RPO provided the connection for Aberdeen mail. From 1 July 1885 there were two Up services, the Limited and the Postal. The Limited ceased on 31 January 1917. The Postal was being called the Up Special Mail during the 1880s but it was not until after World War 1 that it became the Up Special TPO.

Norwich-London Travelling Post Office
See the entry for the London-Norwich TPO.

Norwich Sorting Tender
Commenced as a Norwich-Ely service on 2 August 1869. Extended to London, via Cambridge, by 1893. Rerouted via Ipswich in March 1929 and became the East Anglian TPO.

*Penzance-Bristol Travelling Post Office
See the entry for the Bristol-Penzance TPO.

Penzance-Derby Travelling Post Office
See the entry for the Derby-Penzance TPO.

Perth & Aberdeen Sorting Carriage
Commenced 1871. Ceased by 1893.

Left: **Train formation plan for the North Western TPO (Night Down) in September 1955.**
Collection RMS Library

Above: **On 24 June 1987 the postal stock of the Peterborough-Crewe TPO, seen at Stamford, consisted of Nos 80408 (nearest camera) and 80306, their first time in traffic in the red and yellow livery.**
Peter Johnson

Centre right: **The Peterborough-Crewe TPO ready to leave Leicester on 24 June 1991; the carriages are Nos 80305 (the wrong way round) and 80408. The locomotive is a Parcels Sector red-liveried Class 47, instead of the then usual Class 31; the Class 47s were to take over on non-electrified services.** *Peter Johnson*

Lower right: **The Lincoln Section of the Peterborough-Crewe TPO arrives at Newark in the rain on 25 June 1987. The sorting carriage is No 80316.**
Peter Johnson

Perth-Dingwall Railway Sorting Carriage
See the entry for the Dingwall-Perth RSC.

Perth-Helmsdale Railway Sorting Carriage
See the entry for the Highland Sorting Carriage.

Peterborough District Sorting Carriage
Commenced between Peterborough and London, via
Ely, on 15 September 1858. Became a TPO in 1867,
performing the same work. Superseded by the
Peterborough ST 2 August 1869.

Peterborough Sorting Tender
Commenced 2 August 1869 by taking over the
duties of the Peterborough RPO. Ceased 3 June
1916.

*Peterborough-Carlisle Travelling Post Office
Peterborough-Crewe TPO extended to Carlisle.
Commenced 30 September 1991, routed via Derby
and Crewe.

Peterborough-Crewe Travelling Post Office
See the entry for the Crewe-Peterborough TPO.

**Plymouth & Bristol Travelling Post Office (Foreign
Mails)**
Commenced August 1869. Probably ceased in the
1920s.

Plymouth-Bristol Travelling Post Office
See the entry for the Bristol-Plymouth TPO.

Portsmouth Sorting Carriage
Operated between Southampton and Portsmouth
from 1 August 1865. Ceased 6 October 1923.

Preston-Glasgow Railway Sorting Carriage
See the entry for the Glasgow-Preston RSC.

Preston-Whitehaven Travelling Post Office
The Whitehaven & Carnforth ST extended to Preston
from 26 July 1926. Extended to Stalybridge from
3 January 1965.

Rugby & Birmingham Sorting Carriage
Commenced January 1860. Date of withdrawal
unknown.

Rugby & Leeds Railway Post Office
Commenced October 1852. United with the York &
Newcastle RPO to form the Midland Day RPO from
1 June 1862.

Rugby & Newcastle Railway Post Office
Commenced 1845. Routed to Tamworth and
amalgamated with the Gloucester & Tamworth RPO
to form the Midland RPO from 1852.

St Pancras & Derby Sorting Tender
See the entry for the Derby & St Pancras ST.

Scarborough & Whitby Sorting Carriage
These two places were possibly served by a duty from
York during the 1860s.

Shrewsbury & Aberystwyth Sorting Carriage
Commenced 1883. Became the Aberystwyth-
Shrewsbury SC from 8 September 1930. Ceased
22 September 1939.

Shrewsbury & Crewe Sorting Carriage
Commenced 1 April 1891. Combined with the
Normanton & Stalybridge TPO to form the
Shrewsbury & Normanton TPO from 1 January 1893.

Shrewsbury & Hereford Sorting Carriage
Commenced 1 March 1885. Amalgamated with the
Shrewsbury & Tamworth SC from 28 February 1902.

Shrewsbury & Tamworth Railway Post Office
Commenced January 1857. Known as a TPO from
circa 1868 and as an SC from *circa* 1883. Joined
with the Shrewsbury & Hereford SC and became
the Tamworth & Hereford SC from 1 March
1902.

Shrewsbury-London Travelling Post Office
See the entry for the London-Shrewsbury TPO.

Shrewsbury-Stafford Sorting Carriage
A temporary service which operated in 1985 to cover
the York-Shrewsbury TPO whilst Crewe Station was
closed for track layout rationalisation. During the
closure mail handling took place at Stafford. *En
route* for Stafford the SC was conveyed with the
Shrewsbury-York and the Cardiff-Crewe TPOs; in
the reverse direction with the Crewe-Cardiff TPO
only, the York-Shrewsbury TPO's route avoiding
Stafford. The dates of operation were 3 June-19 July
1985.

Shrewsbury-Tamworth Sorting Carriage
Commenced 6 July 1914. Ceased 28 February 1917.

Shrewsbury-York Railway Sorting Carriage
Created 4 October 1920 by the division of the York-
Cardiff to give this duty and the Crewe-Cardiff SC.
Became a TPO on 14 April 1930.

South Eastern Travelling Post Office
Commenced as the South Eastern RPO on 1 May
1860. The service operated between London Bridge
and Dover until 1866 when it was diverted to Cannon
Street. Known as a TPO from 1870. The London
terminal reverted to London Bridge in 1968 but was
transferred to Victoria shortly afterwards. Ceased
18 February 1977.

Above: **On 20 June 1991 the Lincoln Section of the Peterborough-Crewe TPO arrived at Nottingham with Nos 80321 (next to loco) and 80306 separated by a BG.** *Peter Johnson*

Right: **The Plymouth-Bristol TPO arriving at Exeter St David's on 19 July 1958. Examination with a glass reveals that the door adjacent to the apparatus is opened and someone is standing in it!** *R. C. Riley*

Below: **Taken on 13 May 1988, this photograph shows the empty stock of the South Wales TPO *en route* from Swansea to Carmarthen and records the last occasion the TPO carried passenger accommodation.** *S. K. Miles*

South Wales Sorting Carriage (North Mail)
Commenced 1 March 1884. Operated between Gloucester and New Milford as a feeder and distributor of the Midland RPO. Ceased 27 October 1923.

*South Wales Travelling Post Office
Commenced 3 March 1869, under the control of the Surveyor of South Wales District, Francis Freeling, father of a later Postmaster-General, staffed by two Gloucester men and one from Swansea. Writing in 1925 and then aged 78, a retired staff member recalled that he had joined the TPO soon after it had started, as a junior on apparatus duty, rising to take charge on £1 1s 0d (£1.05) a week, plus 3s (15p) a trip. As with the South Wales SC (North Mail) the route was between Gloucester and New Milford.

The South Wales TPO became an ST in 1873, but was known as a TPO again from the turn of the century. By 1924 Carmarthen was the western terminus; on 13 July 1925 the service was diverted to Bristol, when it was still operated by Gloucester-based men who travelled to Bristol to take up their duties! Between 1946 and 1969 the TPO operated only as far as Milford Haven but the service reverted to Carmarthen from February 1969. From 3 October 1988 Swansea became the Welsh terminus and Paddington the English.

South Western District Sorting Carriage
Commenced, between Waterloo and Southampton, April 1860. Ceased 14 June 1869.

South Western Sunday Sorting Tender
Commenced 20 April 1850. Ceased June 1863.

South Western Travelling Post Office (Day)
Commenced 1866. Extended to Dorchester 30 June 1890. Operated via Bournemouth after June 1901. From 26 November 1923 the service was cut back to Bournemouth. Ceased September 1940.

South Western Travelling Post Office (Night)
Commenced, between Waterloo and Southampton, 19 August 1862 as an RPO. Extended to Dorchester in 1876. Bournemouth was served by a branch working from 1 October 1910. From 1 July 1915 the whole train was routed via Bournemouth. The service was extended to Weymouth from 27 November 1961. Ceased 13 May 1988.

Stafford & Liverpool Sorting Carriage
Commenced 18 April 1865. Ceased *circa* 1880s.

Stafford-Shrewsbury Sorting Carriage
See the entry for the Shrewsbury-Stafford SC.

Above left: **The South Western TPO awaits departure from Waterloo on 9 December 1985.** *Chris Wilson*

Top: **The Up Special TPO waits to leave Aberdeen on 26 April 1983.** *Mick Howarth*

Above: **Loading the Up Special TPO at Glasgow on 10 July 1989.** *Derek V. Crowe*

Right: **LMS No 30216 in use on the Up Special. The additional lighting above the sorting frame is particularly noticeable.** *GPO Newsroom*

Left: **A well-laden Whitehaven-Huddersfield TPO on 6 September 1985. The supervisor deals with paperwork whilst behind him registered letters receive attention.** *Peter Johnson*

Below: **Stock for the York-Shrewsbury TPO being shunted at York on 14 July 1983.** *W. A. Sharman*

Bottom: **The Yorkshire TPO at St Pancras on 28 November 1994.** *Peter Johnson*

Stalybridge-Whitehaven Travelling Post Office
The Preston-Whitehaven TPO extended to Stalybridge from 3 January 1965. Extended to Huddersfield from 2 January 1966.

Tamworth & Hereford Sorting Carriage
The Shrewsbury & Hereford SC and the Tamworth & Shrewsbury SC amalgamated from 25 February 1902. Ceased 1914 when the Hereford-Shrewsbury portion was discontinued, the remainder becoming the Shrewsbury-Tamworth RSC.

Tamworth-Lincoln Sorting Carriage
See the entry for the Lincoln-Tamworth SC.

Tamworth-Shrewsbury Sorting Carriage
See the entry for the Shrewsbury-Tamworth SC.

Truro & Falmouth Sorting Tender
Commenced June 1864. Ceased 1916.

Up Special Mail Travelling Post Office
The renamed Up Postal working of the North Western TPO. The name is first known to have been used in 1886.

Up Special Travelling Post Office
The Special Mail and Postal duties of the North Western TPO were amalgamated in 1917 to give the Up Special TPO. This was the most famous of the TPOs, being the biggest and travelling the longest distance. When the author travelled on it on 9 February 1984 it consisted of seven sorting carriages, five stowage vans and a BG; it had a staff of 53 at Crewe and a further 15 joined it at Birmingham. From 16 May 1988 included the Shrewsbury-London TPO from Rugby. Became a Glasgow-Euston service from October 1988. Ceased 14 May 1993.

Up Special Travelling Post Office (Birmingham Section)
Ran for five nights, between Crewe and Birmingham, from 24 February 1986, during the Proof House Junction bridge renewal.

Up Special Travelling Post Office (Edinburgh Section)
With the establishment of the Up Special TPO in 1922 the Up duty of the Carlisle-Edinburgh SC became the Up Special TPO Edinburgh Section. It ran as a bag tender from 1924. From 1 October 1945 until 7 October 1946 it ran as a TPO again, substituting for the Edinburgh Section of the Caledonian TPO which was not restored from its wartime break until the latter date. At this time it became known as the Edinburgh-Carstairs Bag Duty. In the 1950s parcels vans were substituted for the TPO stock used formerly. Although no mail was sorted, the staff carried a datestamp for administrative purposes and late mail was usually accepted and postmarked. Replaced by the Edinburgh-Carlisle TPO from 3 October 1988.

Up Special Travelling Post Office (Glasgow Section)
The Glasgow Section of the North Western TPO Special Mail probably ran throughout its life; the portion continued after the creation of the Up Special TPO, in 1917, but was not named the Glasgow Section of the Up Special TPO until 1922. Ceased 14 May 1993.

West Cornwall Sorting Tender
Commenced 1 March 1884 operating between Penzance and Truro. Ceased 1892.

Whitehaven Sorting Tender
Commenced between Whitehaven and Carnforth in 1875. Extended to Preston 26 July 1926.

Whitehaven & Carnforth Sorting Carriage
See the entry for the Carnforth & Whitehaven TPO.

Whitehaven-Huddersfield Travelling Post Office
See the entry for the Huddersfield-Whitehaven TPO. On 5 September 1985 carried accommodation for a press party from Workington to Manchester Victoria and hauled by ex-LMS Class 5 4-6-0 No 4767 *George Stephenson* as far as Carnforth; the event was to celebrate the 350th anniversary of the Post Office.

Whitehaven-Preston Travelling Post Office
See the entry for the Preston-Whitehaven TPO.

Whitehaven-Stalybridge Travelling Post Office
See the entry for the Stalybridge-Whitehaven TPO.

York & Scarborough Sorting Carriage
Commenced 1 July 1899. Ceased 1928.

York-Cardiff Travelling Post Office
See the entry for the Cardiff-York TPO.

York-Newcastle Travelling Post Office
Commenced as an RPO 1 July 1853. Incorporated into the Midland RPO Day 1 June 1862. Re-established as a TPO February 1873. Extended to Normanton 1895 and became the North Eastern TPO Day Mail.

York-Shrewsbury Railway Sorting Carriage
See the entry for the Shrewsbury-York RSC.

Yorkshire Travelling Post Office
St Pancras to Newcastle, commenced 3 October 1988. Until May 1990 combined with the Midland TPO from Derby to Newcastle. Last run on 26 May 1995.

3. TPO Rolling Stock

The story of TPO coaching stock begins with the converted horsebox used on the Grand Junction Railway for the experimental service of 1838. The carriage was provided by the railway company at the behest of the Post Office and established a precedent which still applies today, so that the fleet of vehicles applied exclusively to postal use is owned and maintained by British Rail. Throughout the years since 1838 the constructional techniques used on postal stock have usually reflected those used by the railway companies on their passenger vehicles. This did not necessarily mean that the older carriages were withdrawn very quickly; some six-wheeled stock continued in service well into the current century. Speaking in 1899 a supervisor on the Great Western TPO, a Mr King, commented 'I can assure you that working in the TPO in the '60s was a terrible hardship. The carriages were short in length as well as dwarfish in height, and owing to the fact that bogie wheels were not then in vogue, the vibration was intolerable.' At that time Mr King had 40 years' service on TPOs, including 21 years on the Bangor & Leeds RPO.

For postal purposes there were, and are, obviously some differences. The sorting frames, minimal glazing and wider sliding doors are noticeably traditional to the TPO. Until recently special liveries were also applied, although to most members of the public, the most outstanding feature was the exchange apparatus and the late posting box. On many vehicles the latter was a box which was hung on the outside of the carriage while it was being loaded or unloaded. Only in later vehicles was the posting slot an integral part.

Right from the early days it was seen that separate vehicles were needed for stowage as well as sorting. Communications between vehicles was a problem until 1857 when the Midland Railway offered to conduct an experiment for the GPO. The following minute, in the Post Office Archives, was addressed to the Postmaster-General:

'The Midland Company having offered to establish a means of communication between the Travelling Post Office and the Tender which contains the Mail Bags so as to enable the Guard to pass from one to the other while the train is in motion, I instructed Mr Edward Page to accept the offer, and Your Grace will perceive that the proposal has now been carried into effect.

'As this is the first instance in which the Department has obtained a means of communicating between the carriages, it is very satisfactory to find that the experiment has been successful, and in all probability great advantage will result from the facilities thus offered for obtaining greater space for sorting &c during the progress of the Train.'

Thus was the concept of corridor connections between carriages introduced to Britain's railways. Some have made a claim on behalf of Queen Victoria's LNWR-built Royal Train of 1869 but even the LNWR recognised the prior claim of the GPO for in February 1911 it wrote to the latter, referring back to 1859:

'I now learn from our Carriage Superintendent that it is quite correct that gangways were first introduced in connection with the "Travelling Post Office" vehicles, and eventually brought into common use for general passenger traffic, as far as this Company is concerned.'

To make the best use of the space available in the early four-wheeled vehicles the gangways were placed off-centre. As larger and more modern vehicles entered service they retained this feature so that they could be operated with the older cars. This sometimes caused problems when stock was returned from servicing the wrong way round and arrangements had to be made to turn the vehicles concerned. It also prevented through communication with other, centre gangway, stock which might be running with the postal vehicles. This distinction was to remain until the BR Mk 1 postal stock was introduced from 1959.

As the railway network developed, the Post Office entered into agreements with each company regarding the carriage of mails. Where sorting was required, the

Above left: **Brake stowage tender No 80455 at West Ealing on 9 June 1983; the vehicle was built at Wolverton in 1959.** *Alex Dasi-Sutton*

Left: **The second batch of brake stowage tenders had smaller windows, as shown on No 80456, built at York in 1968.** *Post Office*

Diagram of the 1959-built brake stowage vans.
Peter Johnson Collection

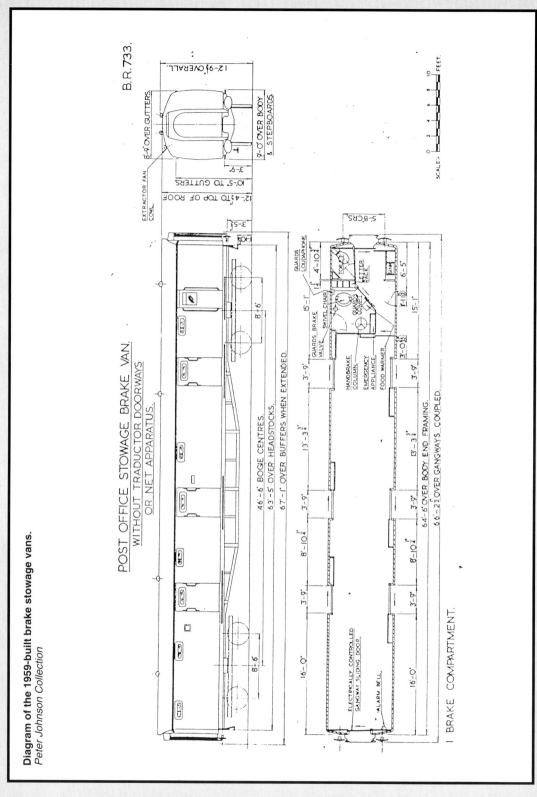

POST OFFICE STOWAGE BRAKE VAN.
WITHOUT TRADUCTOR DOORWAYS
OR NET APPARATUS.

B.R.733.

company was to provide suitable vehicles. They were not permitted to use those of another company, so when the Scottish mails reached Carlisle, for example, they had to be transferred from LNWR stock to that provided by the Caledonian Railway. This particular arrangement lasted until 1885, when the Scottish mails were accelerated, and the companies were able to co-operate in providing the West Coast Joint Stock for postal purposes.

Some details of TPO rolling stock follows, along with some notes on the vehicles which have been preserved.

British Rail

When BR was established in 1948 the postal fleet consisted mainly of vehicles built since the railway Grouping of 1923. There were, however, still some pre-Grouping rolling stock in existence, kept in reserve.

When new construction was required during the 1950s the LMS pattern of vehicle was used, 30 new coaches being built at Wolverton between 1948 and 1958. By this time steps were being taken to withdraw the older vehicles and replace them by new ones, using where possible designs and techniques developed for the Mk 1 passenger coaching stock. The first builds of Mk 1 TPO stock had much larger windows than previously.

The first of the new vehicles entered service on the Great Western TPO on 19 October 1959. Internally the new coaches were little different from their predecessors. There was, however, one major change, which arose from the decision to fit centre gangways instead of the off-centre gangways which had been a feature of so many earlier vehicles.

Eight stowage vans were built with flat ends and fitted with off-centre gangways so that they could work with the older vehicles then running on the Midland TPO. Centre gangways were fitted by 1973.

Nine brake stowage vans were built for use on the Great Western TPO and the Up and Down Specials. They enabled these trains to be made up exclusively of postal vehicles.

In 1995 the purpose-built TPO fleet consists of 123 vehicles: 84 POS (now designated NS5), 36 POT (NT5) and 3 BPOT (NU5). To keep track of the vehicles the TPO Section maintains an availability board at its Mount Pleasant offices. At this time the 1959-built cars are becoming life-expired; because they have only short-letter sorting frames they are non-standard and incompatible with current sorting practice. The last ones are in service on the East Anglian TPO — they are early candidates for withdrawal.

All TPO stock is dual-heated and air-braked. Most of the fleet is capable of operating at 100mph although most services are scheduled to have a maximum speed of 90mph, it having been found that sorting becomes extremely difficult at higher speeds, having a detrimental effect on accuracy.

For the benefit of the staff, the vehicles have toilets, electric water heaters, ovens and wardrobes. The carriages are pressure ventilated and a great deal of effort has gone into providing adequate draught exclusion. To this end the gangway doors are operated electrically and close automatically 7sec after being opened. The door-control push button is placed so that a laden postman can use his elbow to operate it. The opening of a door in one carriage automatically opens that in the adjoining vehicle.

A cast plate was fitted to each side of No 80320 on its being named *The Border Counties* to publicise the launch of the Carlisle-Peterborough TPO in 1991. Something of a celebrity, this carriage was one of the first to be painted in the red and yellow livery and was in

Left: **The interior of No 80400, showing the apparatus net releasing lever on the left.** *Post Office*

Left: **No 80439 was rebuilt from an SK at Wolverton in 1976, when it was the last BR stowage van built; it has a much smaller window in the connecting door. Seen at Derby on 26 June 1987.** *Peter Johnson*

Left: **Stowage van No 80408 seen at Stamford on Peterborough-Crewe TPO duty on 24 June 1987, its first night in traffic in the red and yellow livery. It was rebuilt from a BSK at York in 1966/7.** *Peter Johnson*

Diagram of stowage vans converted from BSKs in 1966/7; the off-centre gangway allowed these vehicles to work with pre-Nationalisation stock.
Peter Johnson Collection

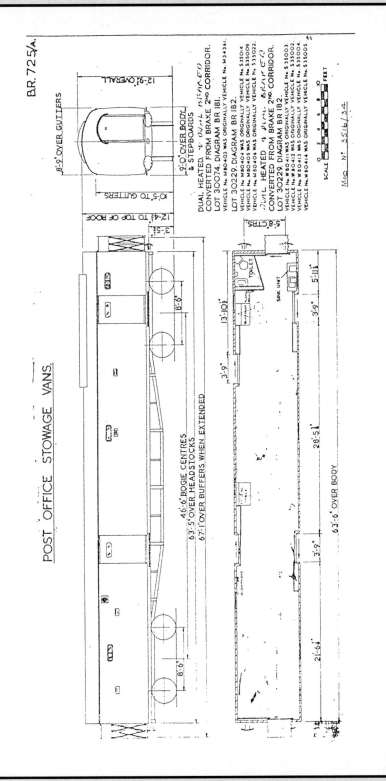

POST OFFICE STOWAGE VANS.

B.R. 725/A.

12'-9½" OVERALL

8'-9" OVER GUTTERS

9'-0" OVER BODY & STEPBOARDS

10'-5" TO GUTTERS

12'-4½" TO TOP OF ROOF

3'-5½"

8'-6"

8'-6"

46'-6" BOGIE CENTRES

63'-5" OVER HEADSTOCKS

67'-1" OVER BUFFERS WHEN EXTENDED

5'-8" CTRS.

13'-10½"

3'-9"

TOILET

SINK UNIT

5'-11½"

3'-9"

21'-6½"

28'-5½"

3'-9"

63'-6" OVER BODY

DUAL HEATED 'B' ONLY DETAILED
CONVERTED FROM BRAKE 2ND CORRIDOR.
LOT 30074. DIAGRAM BR 181.
VEHICLE № M80403 WAS ORIGINALLY VEHICLE № M34361.
LOT 30229. DIAGRAM BR 182.
VEHICLE № M80404 WAS ORIGINALLY VEHICLE № 535014
VEHICLE № M80405 WAS ORIGINALLY VEHICLE № 535009
VEHICLE № M80406 WAS ORIGINALLY VEHICLE № 535022.

DUAL HEATED 'A' DUAL BRAKE 'B' (?)
CONVERTED FROM BRAKE 2ND CORRIDOR.
LOT 30229. DIAGRAM BR 182.
VEHICLE № W80411 WAS ORIGINALLY VEHICLE № 535003
VEHICLE № W80412 WAS ORIGINALLY VEHICLE № 535002.
VEHICLE № W80413 WAS ORIGINALLY VEHICLE № 535004
VEHICLE № W80414 WAS ORIGINALLY VEHICLE № 535005

SCALE 2 1 0 1 2 3 4 5 6 7 8 FEET

MoD № 3516/34

the *Night Mail II* filming set; it also worked on 30 May 1995, the first night of the North East TPO (Down). On 20 June 1995 Penzance-based No 80327 was named *George James*. Mr James is a retired TPO sorter who had worked on TPOs for 44 years and other sorting cars are also to be named after long-serving staff.

Other stock is also allocated to postal duties, BGs (gangwayed full brakes) and GUVs (general utility vehicles), used for stowage. A total of 11 Super BGs — conversions of BGs to Royal Mail requirements to carry containers — were introduced in 1995. The 'new' vehicles have high-security roller shutter doors, steel non-slip floors and a segregated shunter's compartment. Nine vehicles were delivered on 9 January 1995, the others on 20 January. A total of 83 vehicles are to be converted to this standard. No less than 74 GUVs are to be similarly upgraded to Super GUV status, the first undergoing trials in 1993 and entering traffic in February 1994. The last is expected to be converted by October 1995. They are all turned out in Royal Mail livery.

There are also 10 former gangwayed newspaper vans (NL5) converted for stowage, to replace POT/NT5 vehicles. The conversions are designated NP5. A further 22 vehicles are available for conversion if required.

An innovation for postal stock is the conversion of 44 former Class 307 EMU driving trailers to become Propelling Control Vans (PCVs), designed to be attached to the tail of trains which have to change direction to gain depot access, as at Willesden, where trains will be propelled southwards for one mile before gaining the main line. Designed to propel at a maximum speed of 40mph, they will be hauled at speeds of up to 100mph. The PCV driver will call for power from the remote locomotive but will have complete braking facilities. The former passenger area will be converted to Super GUV standard. Prototype conversions were undertaken in 1993. The use of the PCVs will save the cost of a shunting loco and will save time, too.

Caledonian Railway

The Caledonian Railway's first postal carriage was built in October 1848. The company undertook the responsibility of providing the stock for the TPOs which it operated until the creation of the West Coast Joint Stock in 1879. Seven vehicles were taken over for the WCJS, which with one exception were 26ft long. Two were built by the LNWR.

Cambrian Railways

The Cambrian Railway's first sorting carriage entered service in 1888. Numbered 200, it was a 32ft-long six-wheeled carriage. In 1902 it was joined by a 42ft bogie vehicle, No 293. The older car was then kept at Shrewsbury as a spare. Both survived to be renumbered, as 810-11, by the GWR.

Cornwall Railway

Initially the Cornwall Railway hired a sorting carriage from the Bristol & Exeter Railway, an arrangement which did not meet with Post Office approval. Giving way to the pressure applied, the company had its own vehicle built by Shackleford & Co in 1861. It was 28ft 3in long and had a papier mâché body. It remained in service until 31 May 1892. Possibly two vehicles were also modified for postal use in 1862.

Furness Railway

The Furness Railway built two sorting carriages: No 1 in 1887 and No 2 in 1903. The former was 22ft 6in long and the latter was 32ft 6in. Prior to the construction of No 1, a secondhand vehicle of LNWR origin was used.

Glasgow & South Western Railway

The LMS acquired six postal cars from the G&SWR in 1923. They were built between 1887 and 1910, three of them being six-wheelers with 31ft bodies. Prior to undertaking its own construction, the G&SWR had used Caledonian Railway stock.

Grand Junction Railway

Four carriages were built in 1838. They were 16ft long, 7ft high and 7ft 6in wide, weighing 4 tons 2 cwt, unladen, 5 tons laden. They were considered large for the time, the railway company thinking that they would slow the trains down due to wind resistance.

Great Eastern Railway

The GER built 22 postal vehicles, the first in 1886, the last in 1921. No 1 of 1886 had incandescent gas lighting and Westinghouse air brakes. Steam heating was fitted in 1912. Some of the GER vehicles were conversions from third-class carriages or brakes; they were invariably 20 years old on conversion and lasted from 10 to 20 years in postal service. At the Grouping 11 vehicles passed to the LNER, three of these being conversions, which were withdrawn in October 1929, the remainder going in November 1933. Unusually for TPOs, some of these coaches had centre gangways.

Great North of Scotland Railway
This railway built two 27ft sorting carriages in 1886. They had no gangways and lighting was by oil lamps. The spare was a 20ft carriage purchased from the LNWR.

Great Northern Railway
From 1871 the Great Northern Railway built about a dozen postal vehicles. They were constructed at Doncaster, three being designed by H. N. Gresley. A carriage built in 1909, No 1858, contained a number of new features: an integral late fee box, previously these were loose fittings, hung on the outside whilst the TPO was stationary, sometimes being overlooked, with catastrophic consequences; plate glass bottoms to the sorting frames, to show if the frame was empty; gas lighting; steam heating; a gas stove; apparatus on both sides, to eliminate the need to turn the vehicle at York; and linoleum replacing fibre matting on the floor. Some of these features were introduced following a tour of Continental TPOs made by F. H. Williamson of the GPO's Secretary's Office and H. Filmer, Chief Superintendent of the London Postal Service.

The GNR also ran a number of conversions as close-coupled twin-sets. The original six-wheeled vehicles were built *circa* 1889 and the twinning operation took place before World War 1. Some of these sets had apparatus on both sides. Most of the GNR stock had centre gangways. The LNER was to convert some GNR brakes for postal use in 1929; this work was done at Stratford.

Great Western Railway
The first postal vehicles provided by the GWR were bag tenders, used from 1844. They were built to the broad gauge and weighed just over 7 tons. Carriages with a length of 46ft 6in were built in 1883 which were suitable for conversion to standard gauge. Four four-wheeled postal brakes were built in 1891 and 1892. By 1907 they were all in service as passenger brakes. After the gauge conversion of 1892 the GWR built postal stock of three basic styles: clerestory-roofed stock until 1903, elliptical-roofed 68ft/70ft stock until 1910 and steel-panelled stock from 1927 to 1947. Most of the latter were 57ft vehicles, 10 were 50ft, four were 63ft and three were 46ft 6in. On the Ocean Mails run from Plymouth the GWR slipped a postal car at Bedminster for working to Bristol. A complaint was made to the GWR about excessive speed and the severe buffeting postal staff received between Truro and Newton Abbot on 19 August 1946, followed by a further complaint about severe oscillation between Plymouth and Newton Abbot on 9 September that year, perhaps a contributory factor for the first BR standard coaches going to the Great Western TPO in 1959. Afterwards GWR cars were transferred away from their home territory for further use. Those which went to the Southern Region, as reserves, were painted in the Southern's green livery.

Highland Railway
The Highland Railway's list of postal stock ran to 14 vehicles but there was undoubtedly some duplication as new carriages took the numbers of withdrawn vehicles. Nos 1, 2 and 4 were 27ft 6in four-wheelers. No 3 was a 49ft 6in Post Office parcels van built in 1901. Nos 7, 8 and 9 were six-wheeled cars scrapped in 1916-7. Nos 11 and 12 were also six-wheeled cars and had 23ft 6in bodies. Nos 13 and 14 replaced similarly numbered older vehicles, probably in 1914, and were 41ft bogie cars. In 1916 the railway built three new 49ft 6in bogie vehicles, numbered 5, 6 and 10. They had matchboard sides and remained in use until 1961. It is said that they had their origins in a general arrangement drawing obtained from the LNWR, although this was not borne out by their appearance. The original Nos 5, 6 and 10 became passenger luggage vans and then, in LMS days, tool vans. Nine vehicles passed to the LMS in 1923, but only four remained to be renumbered in 1933.

London & Birmingham Railway
A vehicle in use on the London & Birmingham Railway in 1839 was described as being 15ft 3in long, 7ft 7in wide and 6ft 10in high. It had cost £600.

London, Brighton & South Coast Railway
Four four-wheel sorting carriages, 26ft long, were built in 1878. Two were withdrawn in 1899 and one in 1920. Two 48ft carriages were built at Brighton in 1897. They became brake/luggage vans, 928/9, in 1921 and were withdrawn in 1931 and 1933. All six vehicles had clerestory roofs.

London, Chatham & Dover Railway
Two sorting carriages entered service on the LCDR in 1893. The 32ft bodies were mounted on six-wheeled underframes. One was withdrawn in 1917, the other in 1930.

London, Midland & Scottish Railway
From 1929, 68 postal carriages were built to LMS designs. All were built at Wolverton, the same works which produced the LNWR and WCJS fleets. Most of the LMS stock had 60ft bodies, but some were 50ft or 57ft. Two short-bodied vans, of 42ft and 31ft length, were built in 1933; the shorter ran on six wheels and was transferred to parcels duties in 1952, and withdrawn in 1965. Five 60ft vehicles built in 1947 were allocated to the Midland TPO (2) and the Specials; two of the latter for Glasgow workings, whilst the third was for Aberdeen. These postwar vehicles had a 5ft 9in registered letter frame, with a shutter for the adjacent letter frame to give increased registered letter capacity if required. The interior

Right: **No 80316, built at Wolverton in 1961, was performing as the Lincoln Section of the Peterborough-Crewe TPO when seen at Newark on 25 June 1987.**
Peter Johnson

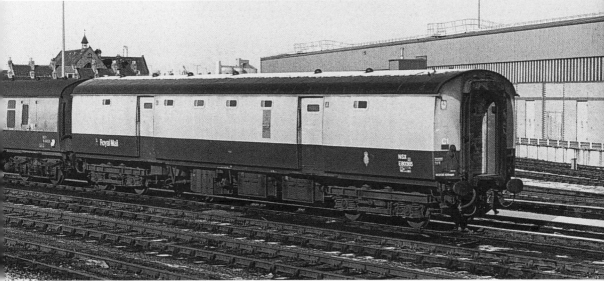

Above: **One of the last batch of sorting vans built at York in 1972/3, No 80365 was photographed at Clifton Carriage Sidings there on 25 February 1986.**
C. J. Tuffs

Right: **The sorting frame side of No 80320 in its *Night Mail II* film livery, with its short-lived red roof, at St Pancras on 26 September 1986. The vehicle was built at York in 1968/9.**
Peter Johnson

Left: **Lincoln is the location for this photograph of sorting van No 80321, built in York in 1968/9; it was about to work the Lincoln Section of the Peterborough-Crewe TPO on 20 June 1991.** *Peter Johnson*

Below: **The Peterborough-Crewe TPO leaving Leicester on 21 June 1991; the sorting carriage is No 80305, showing the current TPO livery style.** *Peter Johnson*

Bottom: **This view of No 80327 shows the current livery applied to the sorting frame side; Coalville Mantle Lane on 21 May 1991.** *Peter Johnson*

colour scheme was duck egg blue, in place of what the staff considered to be 'rather gloomy' green used previously. The first withdrawals from the main fleet were made in 1948, the last being withdrawn by 1978. Thirteen LMS-designed vehicles were transferred to other regions towards the end of their operational lives.

The LMS inherited a large collection of postal vehicles from its constituent companies in 1923. Some of these were very long-lived and survived to see service with British Rail, a few even receiving the blue and grey livery.

London & North Eastern Railway

The LNER inherited 29 postal cars at the Grouping: from the Great Northern, the newest; the North Eastern, built 1902-4 with clerestory roofs; and the Great Eastern, mostly built between 1886 and 1900. All still had gas lighting. As with the later Great Northern Railway vehicles, the LNER postal stock was built to the distinctive designs of Nigel Gresley. Seventeen of these sorting vans were built at York between 1929 and 1937. The first three vehicles entered service on the North Eastern TPO in 1929 and were the first LNER postal cars to have electric lighting. Seven cars built in 1933 went on to the London-York-Edinburgh and also the North Eastern TPOs, the 1929 cars then being transferred to the East Anglian TPO. Two more were allocated to the London-Doncaster TPO in 1936, where they replaced North Eastern Railway stock. A further five vehicles built in 1937 allowed the LNER to complete the withdrawal of its pre-Nationalisation stock. The last TPO car built at York was No 70297, in 1946, when a new body was built on the underframe of the original 1936-built 70297, which had been damaged at Wood Green by enemy action in 1945. After the war Doncaster built six 60ft 1in sorting vans with steel (instead of teak) panelling under BR auspices in 1949 and 1950; they were allocated to the Midland and East Anglian TPOs. Doncaster's first postal vehicle had been a 52ft 4in stowage van built in 1947 for use on the Midland TPO. Two other LNER-design stowage vans were produced by converting other vehicles; a 51ft 1in passenger brake of 1938 was converted after an accident at Gidea Park saw a sorting van and a stowage tender written off in 1947, and a similar vehicle dating to 1930/1, which had become a pigeon van, was converted for postal use in the 1950s. The last LNER postal vehicles withdrawn from service, in 1975, were of the steel-panelled type.

In the 1920s and 1930s the LNER converted 10 former North Eastern Railway and Great Northern Railway vehicles for postal use on the Great Eastern section. The last of these was withdrawn in 1950.

London & North Western Railway

The history of the LNWR postal stock is highly complex. The first vehicles were built following the

Above: **Detail on No 80325.** *Peter Johnson*

Grand Junction Railway TPO experiment in 1838, and 11 vehicles were in use by 1846. One of these survived until 1885 when the Post Office complained about it being used on the Manchester-Crewe service. Some of them, possibly all, were 22ft 6in six-wheeled coaches. More postal stock was built, in 1854 and 1855, with 20ft bodies. In 1879 steps were taken to improve the Scottish mails so the LNWR co-operated with the Caledonian Railway to provide a pool of rolling stock for these services. The pool was to be managed by the West Coast Joint Stock committee to which the LNWR transferred nine postal vehicles. These were up to 25 years old and, with three exceptions, were 22ft 6in long. The remainder were 26ft and 32ft long. The LNWR resumed ownership of some of this stock and took on some of Caledonian origin when they were no longer required by the WCJS. Postal stock was still required by the LNWR for its English and Irish services for which five 32ft vehicles were provided in 1891. By 1899 the railway had 14 32ft carriages in service. At the Grouping 34 vehicles of 42ft and 50ft length were transferred to the LMS.

London & South Western Railway

From 1881 to 1913 18 postal carriages were built for the LSWR. By 1892 five had been built with 32ft

Above: **Interior of No 80327, 1 September 1985.**
Peter Johnson

Left: **The catering facility of No 80327.**
Peter Johnson

Below: **Close-up of the sorting frame of No 80320, seen on 26 September 1986, showing the coiled location fillets used to identify the sorting slots. The inside of the letter box is in the lower left corner.** *Peter Johnson*

Above right: **The registered letter frames of No 80327.** *Peter Johnson*

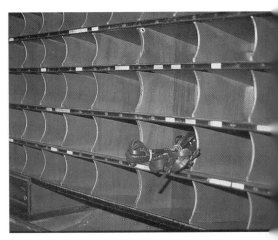

bodies on six-wheel underframes, the last of which was withdrawn in 1933. Bogie stock had 44ft (7), 48ft (4) and 56ft (2) bodies. The whole fleet passed to the Southern Railway in 1923, being renumbered 4901-18. Nos 4902/3 which were 32ft cars built 1881 and 4905, and a 32ft car, built 1889, were withdrawn in 1928, never carrying their Southern numbers. No 4904, built 1886, became departmental 566s in 1931. In 1936/38 seven cars received 'new' underframes from South Eastern & Chatham Railway vehicles. No 4901, withdrawn November 1933, and 4912, withdrawn August 1940, had their bodies grounded at Eastleigh Works and Exmouth Junction respectively. In 1940 No 4911 of 1898 was converted to become an ARP lecture theatre; it then became 1448s. During the war the Southern's TPOs were withdrawn, so several postal vehicles were put to departmental use from 1942. No 4906, built 1900, with 44ft body; No 4916, built 1914, with 56ft body; and 4918, built 1913, also with 56ft body, passed to BR in 1948 and remained in service until *circa* 1960.

Midland Railway

The first Midland Railway TPO vehicles entered service in 1845. They were similar to the contemporary London & Birmingham Railway vehicles, being built by the same builder in Birmingham. Two more carriages were built in 1850 and a further two in 1852. The last two were jointly owned by the Midland, the York & North Midland, the York, Newcastle & Berwick and the North British

Railways, probably because they ran as bag tenders between Newcastle, where connection was made with the Midland TPO, and Edinburgh. Three vehicles built in 1857 were owned solely by the Midland but the North Eastern Railway made a contribution towards their cost. The first of a number of six-wheeled vehicles was built in 1858. A further nine, with 30ft bodies, entered service in 1859. In 1885 two 43ft vehicles were built, then one in 1886, two in 1888, one in 1893 and a further one in 1896. Three 32ft vehicles were also added to the roster in 1885.

The nine 54ft vehicles built in 1907 were the last postal stock to be built by the Midland. All stock used on the Midland TPO was jointly owned by the North Eastern Railway and operated as the Midland & North Eastern Joint Postal Stock. The joint operation continued after the Grouping when the partners were the LMS and the LNER. The vehicles which were used on the Bristol-Derby and the Lincoln-Tamworth services were wholly owned by the Midland Railway.

North British Railway

The first postal vehicles to enter service on the North British Railway were bag tenders, in 1853. They were fitted with apparatus in August 1861 and replaced by new sorting carriages the following month. By 1895 three 23ft 7in carriages had been acquired from the North Eastern Railway. A 28ft 6in vehicle, No 2, built in 1882 was withdrawn in 1920. A 32ft carriage built in 1887, No 5, was withdrawn in 1915. A further 32ft carriage, No 6, entered service in 1891. Nos 5 and 6 had Westinghouse brakes and were piped for vacuum. A 52ft car was built in 1904 and a fifth vehicle followed in 1905.

North Eastern Railway
The operation of the Midland & North Eastern Joint Postal Stock in conjunction with the Midland TPO was the North Eastern Railway's greatest involvement with postal services. A small fleet of TPO carriages was also maintained for local services. A 22ft 9in vehicle of 1897 was later close-coupled to a 24ft vehicle of 1873 and the two operated as a pair. Vehicles of 23ft 7in were built in 1872 and 1876 and later sold to the North British Railway. A 52ft carriage, No 291, was built in 1903 with gas lighting, a net and four traductors. No 333 was a bogie vehicle built in 1910. North Eastern stock remained in use with the LNER until 1933.

South Eastern & Chatham Railway
The SE&CR ran a fleet of 10 postal vehicles, including four sorting carriages built by the South Eastern Railway in 1881, 1883 and 1896 (2) and one by the London, Chatham & Dover Railway in 1893; the three eldest having gangways at one end only. It also operated five 50ft 1in stowage vehicles built under its own auspices in 1904 (3) and 1906. All 10 cars passed to the Southern Railway, becoming Nos 4944-53, in 1923, when the stowage vans were classified as luggage vans. Three of them were restored to postal service as 4954-56 in 1931. The LCDR vehicle, No 4946, was withdrawn in 1930, followed by Nos 4944/5, SER vehicles, in 1933. Nos 4947/8 transferred to departmental use in 1939 and 1940, becoming Nos 1449s and 1537s. The remainder saw service with BR until withdrawal in 1960 and 1961, when 4951 became internal user 081039. It is interesting to note the constructional details of these vehicles which had a teak body frame with mahogany panels; the underframe had wooden headstocks, channel iron bolster cross bars and iron end longitudinals, the rest being of oak.

South Eastern Railway
By 1896 the South Eastern Railway had built 13 postal carriages. The oldest was a four-wheeler built in 1855; three more four-wheelers were built in 1866 and 1868. The 1855 vehicle was transferred to departmental use in 1902. The others were withdrawn in 1906. Five six-wheelers were built in 1859/60 and 1863; four were withdrawn in 1906, the fifth had already been in departmental service since 1902. Two more six-wheeled vehicles were built in 1881 and 1883; they passed to the Southern Railway and were withdrawn in 1933. The only bogie vehicles were 44ft stowage vans built in 1896. In 1939 one of these, No 4947, became an ARP instruction coach, the other passed to departmental service a year later; as Mess & Tool Van No 1537s it remained in use until 1961.

Southern Railway
The postal stock inherited by the SR in 1923 has already been mentioned. Its inherited stock was reasonably long-lived, so it was not necessary for the company to consider providing replacements until the 1930s. A prototype sorting carriage was built at Eastleigh in 1936 and three more similar vehicles appeared in 1939; differences including the provision of a toilet. Four stowage vans also appeared in 1939. All vehicles had 58ft bodies. One of the stowage vans was allocated to the Dover service, the remainder to the Dorchester run. The operating pattern remained the same after BR took over in 1948. The first withdrawal, a stowage van, took place in 1962, possibly due to accident damage. The last duty for these vehicles was on the South Eastern TPO; the end of the TPO on 18 February 1977 brought about their withdrawal. Three have been preserved.

West Coast Joint Stock
In 1879 the LNWR and the Caledonian Railway agreed to pool sufficient postal stock to permit the London-Aberdeen duties to be worked by the same stock throughout. The LNWR supplied nine cars, the Caledonian seven. From 1881 new stock was specially built at Wolverton. A total of 75 postal vehicles had been built, to 23 different diagrams, by 1922. The earliest coaches had 26ft bodies; the latest, built in 1917, measured 64ft. The LMS absorbed both WCJS partners and the joint stock, then 41 vehicles, ceased to be operated separately. The last item of WCJS was withdrawn by BR in 1965.

In 1888 Wolverton built two one-sixth full-size scale models of 32ft and 42ft WCJS sorting carriages for the German postal museum in Berlin. Their fate is not known.

Liveries
Until the introduction of the BR Mk 1 stock, TPO vehicles were usually painted in a variation of the operating company's standard passenger livery, usually incorporating the inscription 'Royal Mail', the royal coat of arms and/or a cipher. The 1838 Act of Parliament 'to provide for the carriage of the Mails by Railways' actually said 'on all carriages to be provided for the service of the Post Office on any such railway there shall on the outside be painted the Royal Arms, in lieu of the name of the owner and the number of the carriage'.

The BR stock was at first painted Post Office red lined in black and yellow and this livery was, with some exceptions, also applied to the pre-Nationalisation stock then still in service. The colour used tended to vary in shade according to the works which applied it, the St Rollox variation being particularly distinctive. The Southern Region continued the Southern Railway practice of painting TPO carriages green to match the passenger stock, applying it to transferred ex-GWR stock also. From

Right: **No 80307 at Inverness prior to working the Up Highland TPO on 24 October 1977.** *Peter Johnson*

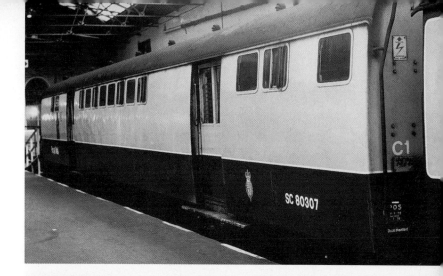

Right: **Crewe is the location of this picture of No 80382 at work in the Birmingham-Glasgow TPO on 17 May 1995.** *Peter Johnson*

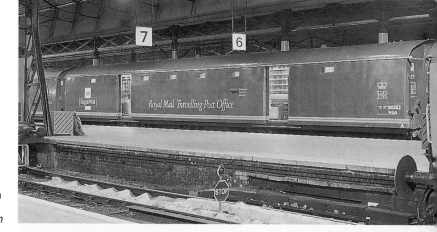

Below: **Named No 80320 in the North East TPO at Peterborough on 30 May 1995, the TPO's first night of operation.** *Peter Johnson*

Above: **TPO stock in the Wembley InterCity Carriage Depot on 22 November 1987.** *Brian Morrison*

1970 the standard blue and grey was applied; this was probably a delayed reaction to the Great Train Robbery and a desire to reduce the TPOs' profile, but the 'Royal Mail' brand, royal crest and red letterbox panel contrived to make these vehicles as distinctive as ever.

In 1986 the eight TPO cars and the BR brake chosen for the *Night Mail II* filming were turned out painted red with yellow lettering and lining, complete with red roofs to aid aerial filming. Some vehicles were also lettered 'Royal Mail Letters'. After this train went into service on the North Eastern TPO it was decided to apply the film livery, with the exception of the red roofs, which quickly became dirty, to the entire fleet. A variation of this livery was later applied to the British Rail parcels stock. From 1990 the postal stock livery was itself further modified by the substitution of white lettering, in different fonts, for the yellow and the introduction of the current Royal Mail crest. Advantage was taken of this modified design to letter some of the vehicles 'Royal Mail Travelling Post Office', the first time public acknowledgement had been given to the purpose of TPO stock.

Preservation

The number of TPO vehicles in preservation is very small and many interesting types have been lost. Constructional details were often common to the story

of carriage development, however, and can therefore be seen in other vehicles which have been saved.

None of the four- and six-wheel TPO vehicles has survived. Some idea of early construction may be obtained from the replica Grand Junction Railway coach built by the LMS for the TPO centenary celebrations in 1938. Until it went on display at the Museum of British Transport, at Clapham, it was stored at Wolverton Works. Since 1975 it has been on show at the National Railway Museum in York, although it spent time at the Birmingham Railway Museum at the Crewe Heritage Centre in 1988.

Another survivor from the TPO centenary exhibition also on display at York is the West Coast Joint Stock No 186, which was built for the accelerated Scottish services of 1885. It was withdrawn and restored to 1885 condition, complete with a Webb radial truck, especially for the exhibition. It is the oldest surviving British TPO vehicle.

Built in 1909, London & North Western Railway No 20 was renumbered 9520 by the LNWR and 3227 and 30244 by the LMS. The latter number, allocated in 1933, lasted until the vehicle was withdrawn in 1961. It was used on the Irish services until 1940 and

Diagram of 1969-built sorting cars.
Peter Johnson Collection

POST OFFICE SORTING VAN
WITH NET APPARATUS.

B.R. 729

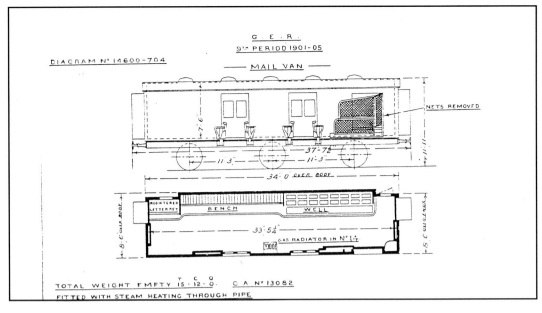

G . E . R .
9ᵀᴴ PERIOD 1901-05

DIAGRAM Nº 14600-704

MAIL VAN

NETS REMOVED

37·7½
11·3
11·3
34·0 OVER BODY

REGISTERED LETTER NET
BENCH
WELL
33·5¼
GAS RADIATOR IN Nº 14

TOTAL WEIGHT EMPTY 15-12-0.   C A Nº 13082
FITTED WITH STEAM HEATING THROUGH PIPE

Above: **Diagram of Great Eastern Railway sorting cars Nos 13 and 14.** *Peter Johnson Collection*

Left: **Detail of the corridor end of a Great Western Railway TPO car.** *L&GRP*

its apparatus was removed in 1945. After withdrawal it was acquired by the Railway Preservation Society and taken to its base at Chasewater, Staffordshire, where it housed the small relics collection. In 1983 it was sold to the Birmingham Railway Museum which now wishes to sell the vehicle, plans to restore and demonstrate it not having been fulfilled.

The Great Western Railway is represented by No 814, a stowage van built in 1940 to replace an identical vehicle which was destroyed in an accident that year. Following the introduction of BR standard stock on the Great Western TPO in 1959, No 814 was transferred to the Southern Region as a spare for the South Western TPO workings. When the standard stock reached these duties in 1972 it became surplus to

postal requirements and was transferred to departmental service. Becoming surplus again, it was sold to the Great Western Society in June 1975. The Society erected lineside apparatus alongside its demonstration line at Didcot in 1973 but it was not until 11 August 1979 that the apparatus was tested with the carriage. The ensemble was first demonstrated to the public on 29 September 1979 and instantly became a popular feature of the Society's open days. In 1987 No 814 was withdrawn for a major overhaul which was not completed until early in 1994, the carriage returning to action at Easter that year.

The only combination of sorting and stowage vans to be preserved together originated with the London & North Eastern Railway. The set belongs to Railway Vehicle Preservations, which acquired the stowage van, No 70268, in 1973. Built as a passenger brake in 1931, around 1960 it was converted to become a PO stowage van, based at Newcastle. The sorting van, No 70294, was built as No 2441 at York in 1937. It was used on East Coast main line services until the 1960s when it was transferred to East Anglia for use on the Norwich-London TPO, replacing Nos 70277 and 70299. The net apparatus was retained for collecting mail from Manningtree — two pouches; Colchester — six pouches; Witham — three pouches; and Chelmsford — six pouches. The empty pouches were returned on the Norwich-London bag tender, with those for

Right: **Great Western Railway sorting car No 835, built for the Great Western TPO in 1905.** *Peter Johnson Collection*

Below: **No 795 was one of three Great Western stowage vans built in 1933.** *J. H. Aston*

Bottom: **Great Western brake stowage van No 813 painted green for service on the Southern Region. Seen at Swindon on 31 August 1965.** *P. H. Swift*

Diagram of GWR brake stowage vans Nos 812-4.
Peter Johnson Collection

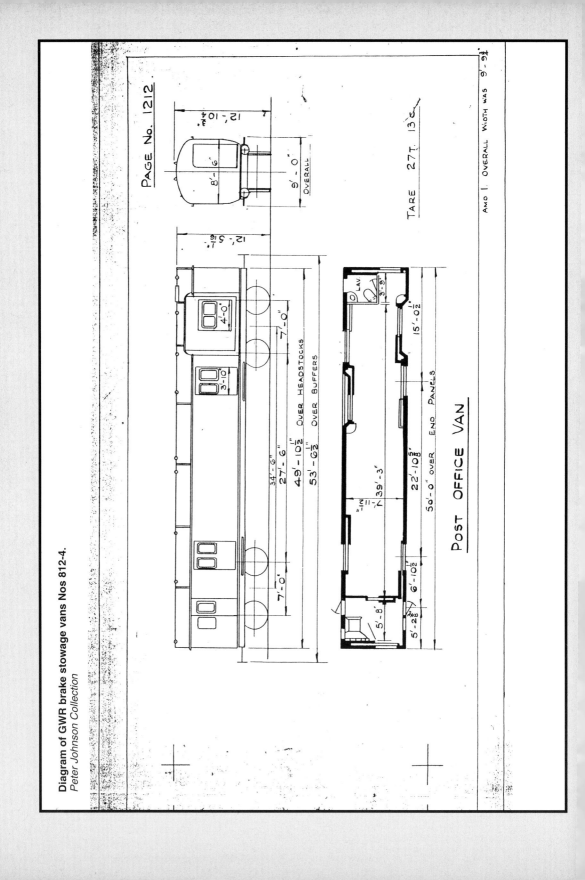

PAGE No. 1212.

12'-10¾"

6"

8'-0"

9'-0"
OVERALL

12'-5⅛"

4'-0"

7'-0"

3'-10

34'-6"

27'-6"

49'-10½" OVER HEADSTOCKS

53'-6½" OVER BUFFERS

7'-0"

LAV.

3'-9

15'-0½"

39'-3"

11'-7½"

22'-10⅝"

50'-0" OVER END PANELS

6'-10½"

5'-8"

5'-2⅝"

POST OFFICE VAN

TARE 27T. 13c.

AMD 1. OVERALL WIDTH WAS 9'-9¾"

Above: **A Great Western Railway passenger brake, built in 1933 with off-centre gangways for connecting to TPO stock.** *Peter Johnson Collection*

Manningtree being put off at Colchester for onward transmission by passenger train. It was sold in 1974 and bought by RVP which moved it to join the stowage van at Rye House power station. By 1976 both had been moved to the Stour Valley Railway at Chappel & Wakes Colne Station in Essex. They moved again, in June 1981, to the Great Central Railway in Leicestershire. Work started on restoration to operational condition immediately and arrangements were made to install the ground apparatus, owned since 1974, at Quorn & Woodhouse station. Tests were carried out in the first week of May 1982 and the first public demonstration took place on the eighth of that month. Leicester Post Office supplied postmen in vintage uniforms and a special postmark was applied to the mail which was put through the apparatus.

A sorting van, No 30225, was built at Wolverton works by the London, Midland & Scottish Railway in 1939 and saw service on the Up and Down Specials and the North Western TPO until 1968. Its nets were then removed and it was transferred to the Manchester-Glasgow SC duty. Purchased by Derby Corporation after withdrawal in 1973 it is now to be seen at the Midland Railway Centre at Butterley, Derbyshire. Before the Trust opened its line, the TPO vehicle served as a museum at Butterley. It is now on show at Swanwick and may be restored to working order as the Trust does own both ground and carriage apparatus.

No 30272 is a similar LMS-design sorting carriage, the only obvious difference being the provision of a toilet compartment; it is owned by the National Railway Museum, being built at Wolverton by BR to an LMS design in 1950. It was withdrawn from service in 1973 and placed in store until the summer of 1984 when it was transferred to the Birmingham Railway Museum.

Of the seven TPO carriages built by the Southern Railway in 1939, three have been preserved. No 4920 is a sorting van; allocated to the South Western TPO until 1972, it was then transferred for use on the South Eastern TPO. It was withdrawn when this service finished in 1977 and is now owned by the National Railway Museum. It is on loan to the Nene Valley Railway at Wansford, Cambridgeshire, and has been fitted out as a museum, one of its custodians being a former member of TPO staff.

Southern Railway sorting van No 4922 had a similar service history to No 4920 but actually ran in the South Eastern TPO on 18 February 1977, the TPO's last night. It is now based at Horsted Keynes on the Bluebell Railway. It has sometimes run in special trains run in conjunction with the Bluebell's railway letter service.

Upon withdrawal in 1977 Southern Railway stowage van No 4958 was bought by the Mid Hants Railway and is located at Ropley where it has been incorporated into a workshop.

At the time of writing only one member of the BR-built fleet has entered preservation. Sorting tender No 80307 was donated by the Post Office to the Severn Valley Railway in 1990. The gift was made to commemorate the 150th anniversary of universal 1d postage, Kidderminster being Rowland Hill's birthplace. No 80307 was built at Wolverton in 1959, without any provision for apparatus. It is kept at Kidderminster and has occasionally been taken out on trips along the railway's line to Bridgnorth. In 1995 plans were being made for a TPO exhibition to be permanently set up in the carriage.

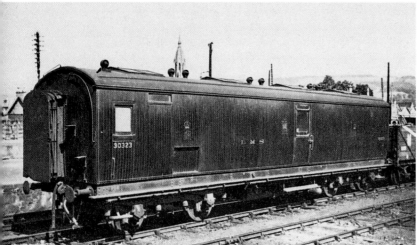

Above: **The apparatus side of LMS No 30323, built by the Highland Railway in 1916.** *Peter Johnson Collection*

Left: **The sorting frame side of No 30323.** *Peter Johnson Collection*

Below left: **LMS tool van No 354398 started life as a Highland Railway postal car.** *W. H. Whitworth*

Above right: **A London & Birmingham Railway carriage, from an engraving made in 1839.** *The Literary World/Post Office*

Below right: **London, Brighton & South Coast Railway No 401 was one of two vehicles built in 1878.** *F. Burtt/National Railway Museum*

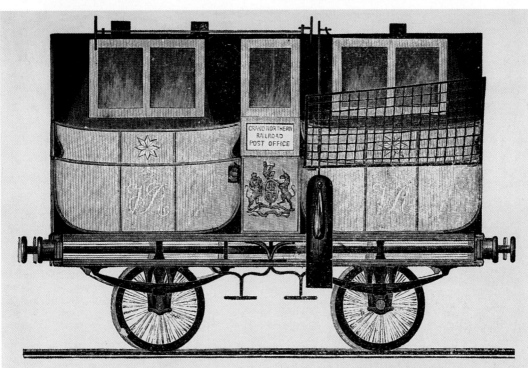

TRAVELLING POST-OFFICE, ON THE LONDON AND BIRMINGHAM RAILWAY.

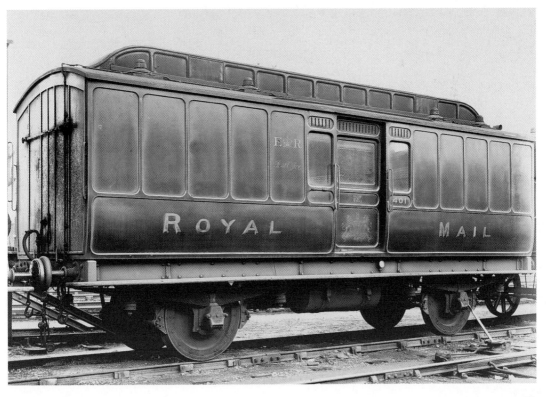

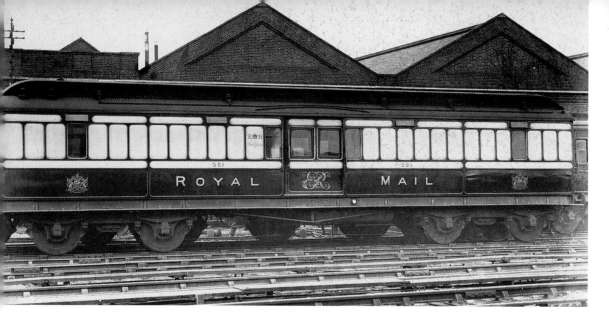

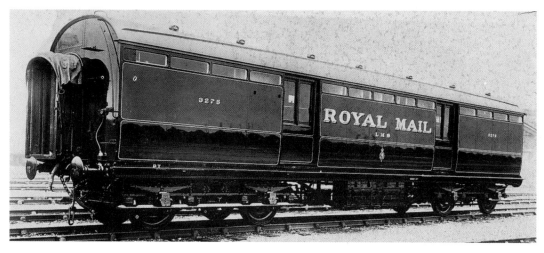

Left: **London, Brighton & South Coast Railway No 351 was built in 1897 and converted to a brake in 1921. It was withdrawn in 1931** *F. Burtt/National Railway Museum*

Centre left: **LMS No 3242 was a 57ft sorting carriage built at Wolverton in 1929.** *F. Moore's Railway Photographs*

Bottom left: **The off-side of LMS No 3275.** *Peter Johnson Collection*

Above right: **LMS No 30235 was a Wolverton-built 60ft vehicle weighing 33 tons. It is shown on the West Coast main line coupled to BR stowage van No 80404, the latter having been built with off-centre gangways to permit its working with pre-Nationalisation stock. It was fitted with centre gangways when the pre-Nationalisation stock was withdrawn.** *Peter Johnson Collection*

Centre right: **LMS No 3275 was a 50ft stowage van built at Wolverton in 1930.** *Peter Johnson Collection*

Below: **LMS-design stowage vans Nos 30279 (built 1950) and 30305 (built 1954) found further use as a store and canteen at a Leicester packing case factory from 1978. They were later removed for scrapping by Vic Berry.** *Peter Johnson*

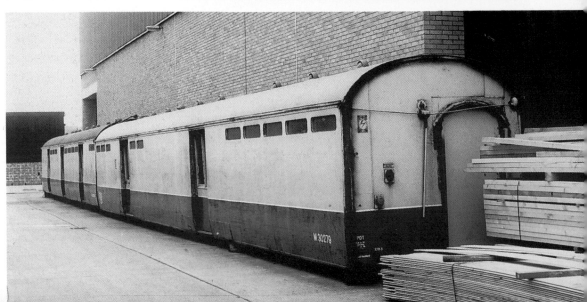

Above: **Built in Wolverton in 1933, 42ft No 30304 was one of a kind and had no internal fittings when built.** *Peter Johnson Collection*

Above right: **Detail of No 30279.** *Peter Johnson*

Below: **York is the location of this unusual view of No 30291, taken in 1952. It had been built in 1939, one of a batch of three. By 1966 it was running with four tractors fitted.** *David Ibbotson*

Below right: **Another interior view of No 2339. This 60ft 1½in carriage was re-numbered 70279 from 1943.**
Ian Allan Library

Right: **The interior of LNER No 2339, built at York in 1929, one of the batch of three sorting carriages built that year. Notable features are the apparatus net lever and the inside of the letter box, both on the right.** *Ian Allan Library*

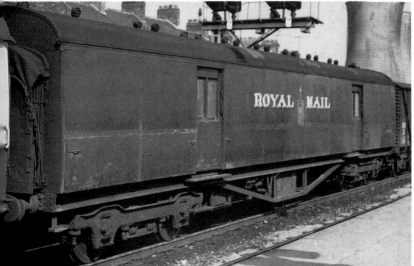

Above: **LNER No 70290 was built in 1933 as No 2155; the picture shows the classic lines of the Gresley design.** *Peter Johnson Collection*

Left: **This steel-panelled 60ft LNER sorting carriage was one of a batch of five built in 1949/50.** *Peter Johnson Collection*

Below left: **Detail of No 70299, an LNER vehicle built in 1937. This 60ft car was first used on the London-Leeds TPO but was later allocated to the Norwich-London TPO/London-Norwich BT duties.** *Peter Johnson Collection*

Bottom right: **A former Midland Railway postal car found a new life at Shepton Mallet after it was no longer required by the Post Office or the railway, but clearly it was not well loved.** *Peter Johnson Collection*

Right: **No 70299** was one of a batch of five cars which also included the preserved **No 70294**, shown here on the Great Central Railway at Loughborough when first restored. *Peter Johnson*

Below: LMS **No 30244**, seen at Carlisle in 1956, was LNWR **No 20**, the vehicle now at the Birmingham Railway Museum. Judging by the panels which had been replaced, it was in a bad way even then. *Real Photos*

Above: **LNWR sorting carriage No 35 posed for the camera. Under LMS and BR ownership it was No 30252.** *Real Photos*

Below: **The interior of LNWR No 35.** *Real Photos*

Right: **Midland & North Eastern Railway Joint Postal Stock was allocated to the Midland TPO. The sorting frame side of No 5 is shown, the vehicle having a connection at one end only.** *Collection F. W. Shuttleworth*

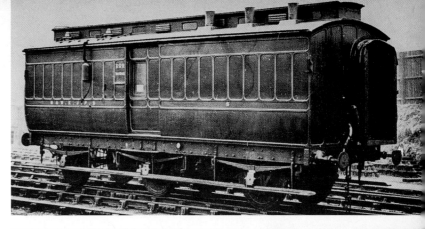

Right: **M&NERJPS No 30284 was built in 1907 by the Midland Railway. It is seen coupled to No 30296.** *Peter Johnson Collection*

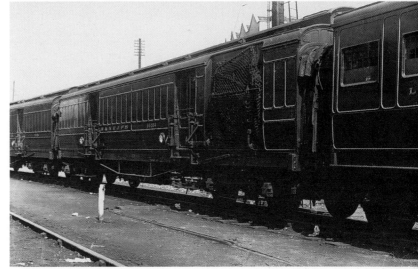

Right: **North Eastern Railway No 1 was built in 1885.** *GPO Newsroom*

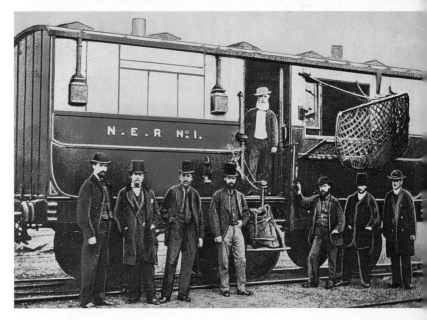

Left: **South Eastern Railway No 350 was a 44ft sorting carriage built in 1896. It was one of a pair and had a gangway at one end only. Renumbered 1449 by the Southern Railway, during the war it became an Air Raid Precautions van, on which duty it was photographed at Wimbledon on 18 October 1946, although it appears to be coupled to a postal vehicle.** *D. Cullum*

Above: **South Eastern & Chatham Railway Nos 691, 693 and 692, later Southern Railway Nos 4951, 4953 and 4952 respectively, were built at Ashford in 1904. No 691 was gangwayed at one end only and the others were apparatus fitted.** *National Railway Museum*

Left: **SECR No 693, as Southern Railway No 4953, seen at Rotherhithe Road on 26 April 1947**. *D. Cullum*

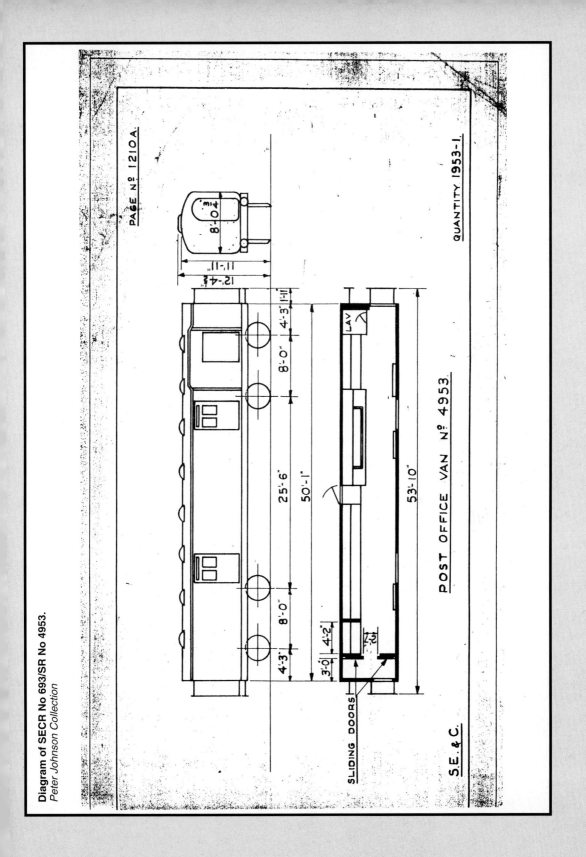

Diagram of SECR No 693/SR No 4953.
Peter Johnson Collection

PAGE Nº 1210A.

QUANTITY 1953-1.

POST OFFICE VAN Nº 4953.

S.E. & C.

LAV

SLIDING DOORS

8'-0"

3'-0"

8'-0¾"

11'-11"

12'-4½"

4'-3"

8'-0"

4'-3" 11'-11"

25'-6"

50'-1"

53'-10"

4'-2"

3'-0"

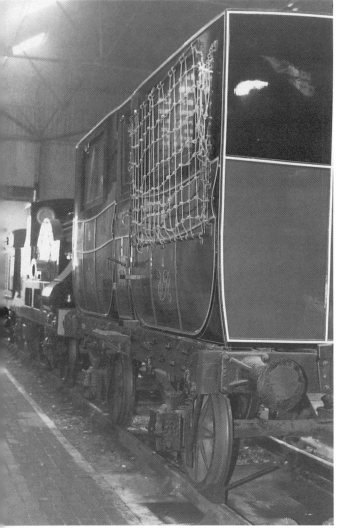

Above: **LMS No 30311, built as West Coast Joint Stock No 184, had had its apparatus net removed when seen at Carlisle in 1956. It was withdrawn in 1958.** *Real Photos*

Left: **The LMS-built replica 1838 London & Birmingham Railway sorting carriage at the Birmingham Railway Museum, Tyseley, on 5 March 1988.** *Peter Johnson*

Below: **Southern Railway No 4920 at Wansford on the Nene Valley Railway.** *Peter Johnson*

Above: **The interior of WCJS No 186.** *Peter Johnson*

Right: **Preserved West Coast Joint Stock No 186 and lineside apparatus at the National Railway Museum on 1 February 1988.** *Peter Johnson*

Below: **LNWR No 20 at the Birmingham Railway Museum, Tyseley, on 5 March 1988.** *Peter Johnson*

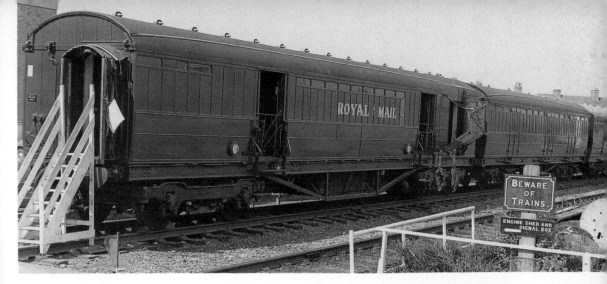

Above left: **GWR 814 being positioned for transfer to the demonstration line at Didcot on 15 April 1995.** *Peter Johnson*

Below left: **At the Great Central Railway's Quorn & Woodhouse Station GCR 4-4-0 No 506** *Butler Henderson* **hauls the LNER TPO set past the apparatus on 30 October 1982.** *John Stretton*

Above: **The LNER TPO set on display at Loughborough Central on the Great Central Railway in May 1982.** *Peter Johnson*

Centre right: **The National Railway Museum is the owner of LMS No 30272, seen at the Birmingham Railway Museum on 5 March 1988.** *Peter Johnson*

Lower right: **The interior of No 30272.** *Peter Johnson*

4. Working the Apparatus

The historical background to apparatus working has been covered earlier; now the actual operation is described. TPO apparatus transferred mail from the ground to the TPO and vice versa. For either function to work, three items of equipment were required: the ground apparatus, the carriage apparatus and the pouches in which the mails were exchanged.

The pouches were made of stout leather with four flaps that could be wrapped over the contents. Leather straps passing over and around the pouch secured them. An empty pouch weighed around 20lb. Loaded, a pouch could weigh up to 60lb. The 1939 rule book had the following to say about their make-up:

'5.   *Making up pouches.* The contents of the bags should be carefully shaken into position so that the bags can be packed neatly in the pouch and

completely covered by the leather. When only one bag is enclosed in a pouch, the bottom of the bag should be laid at the lower end of the pouch, and the top of the bag should be turned over the seal. When two or more bags are enclosed in the same pouch they should be laid with the top of the second bag to the bottom of the first and so on alternately. The pouch should be packed in such a way that when suspended on the standard it will hang vertically. The small cross-straps should invariably be buckled, and the main strap should be passed through at least three of the five loops and round the pouch once only before buckling it; the remaining portion of the main strap should be carefully tucked in. The pouch should be made up carefully and tightly to prevent the contents shifting at the moment of transfer into the TPO, but the straps should not be pulled so tight as to damage the correspondence.'

Obviously mail which was put through the apparatus received quite a buffeting and anything deemed unsuitable for apparatus working was transferred away

Left: **Preparing the pouch on the Great Northern Railway, 1910.** *H. Lazenby/Real Photos*

Below: **Apparatus working forerunner,** *circa* **1838.** *Alan Violet Collection*

Above: **Attaching the pouch to the traductor.**
H. Lazenby/Real Photos

Right: **Putting out the traductors; notice the safety barrier, the pull-string for use if the spring mechanism failed to return the traductor inboard automatically, and the lamp to illuminate the operation at night.** *H. Lazenby/Real Photos*

if possible. A cachet reading 'not to be delivered by apparatus' has been recorded used, possibly by the Stores Department, in 1901. From 1902 until 1930 a series of adhesive labels was affixed to appropriate items to explain any delay in delivery. The oldest labels read 'This Packet has been diverted from the usual route, as it appeared to be too fragile for transfer by Mail Apparatus'. Later versions were modified with the word 'unsuitable' substituted for 'too fragile'. The mail bag designated for such items led to this enquiry from a trainee hanging bags on the Great Western TPO Down: 'Is Liskeard Fragile anywhere near Liskeard?'

To transfer mail to a TPO the pouch was mounted on a lineside standard. The placing of these in relation to the track was critical, especially as the clearance between a loaded standard and a train was less than 18in. For this reason the heads of the 10ft tall standards were turned away from the trackside when not in use. The rule book said:

'2.   *Safety Precautions.* In the interests of safety lineside apparatus officers should never pass BETWEEN the apparatus and the line on which the Mail train passes, on the way to or from the standard. They should always pass at the back of the apparatus. After the Mail train has passed, the standard should be turned to the out-of-working position immediately and the net frame closed. The latter operation must be performed while standing

between the wood and iron frames, and the frame should be eased down gently.'

Regarding the use of the lineside apparatus:

'6.   *Suspending and turning pouches to the line.* Pouches should be carried to the standard on the shoulder, and placed on the platform near to the pin to which they are to be attached. The platform should then be mounted and the pouch raised by the drop-strap to meet the pin. When the drop-strap is at the correct height, the right hand should be moved from the drop-strap and placed over the top of the pin box to guide the strap on to the pin and to help to keep the operator steady.

'The standard should be turned carefully to prevent the pouch moving along the pin, and after the pouches have been turned to the line they should be examined to see that the drop-strap is well on the

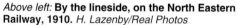

Above left: **By the lineside, on the North Eastern Railway, 1910.** *H. Lazenby/Real Photos*

Left: **At Llandudno Junction in 1929.** *Real Photos*

Above: **Attaching the pouch.** *Real Photos*

Above right: **Waiting for the train.** *Real Photos*

pin and held firmly by the jaws of the pin box. The standard should always be turned on and off by means of the handle, while the operator is standing on the ladder.

'If after having turned the suspended pouches to the line it is observed that an approaching train is not the Mail train, no attempt should be made to reverse them unless it is evident that the standard can be turned to the out-of-working position before the engine of the approaching train reaches the apparatus. No attempt should be made to turn the standard while the operator is on the platform — this must be done while standing on the ladder.'

Sometimes there would be several standards at one location. The postman would attach the pouches to the standards about 10min before the train was due, usually receiving a warning gong signal from the nearest signalbox. If there was no warning signal then the pouches were not turned to the line until 5min

before the TPO was due to pass. At night the suspended pouches had to be illuminated by an oil handlamp held by the trackside postman.

The pouch was removed from its standard by the carriage net, that distinctive feature of TPOs for over a century. The net had to be lowered at just the right moment if the operation was to be successful. Too soon or too late and serious damage could be done to the net (and the train) by lineside structures; the failure to effect the exchange was the least of the operator's problems. Across the mouth of the net a wire was stretched to pull the pouch off the standard; it would drop into the net and roll into the carriage. While the net was extended a warning bell sounded continuously, and a barrier was placed in the corridor connection to protect unwary staff from flying pouches.

To transfer mail to the lineside the pouch was attached to a traductor. There could be as many as four of these attached to the side of the carriage. One would be situated either side of a doorway. The operator would have to lean out of the doorway to attach the pouch, a hazardous move, for which a safety bar was provided. When extended, the arm of the traductor suspended the pouch 3ft away from the carriage and about 5ft from the ground. The impact of the pouch being detached caused the spring-loaded traductor to return inboard. If the spring failed, a rope allowed the job to be done manually.

Below left: **At Harrow & Wealdstone, after the war, when double summer time was in operation. Notice the strings holding the bags in position. The postman, who should be standing in the hut doorway, obviously didn't want to have his photograph taken.** *C. R. L. Coles*

Right: **Lineside apparatus, showing the warning board.** *Peter Johnson Collection*

Below right: **A period piece at High Barnet, before World War 1.** *Collection C. J. Whitehead*

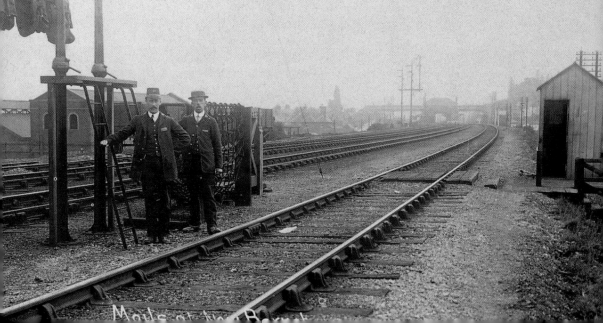

Mails at

The pouch was removed from the traductor by a wire stretched across the mount of the ground net. Because it was so close to the trackside the side of the net nearest the track was collapsed down when not in use. The following 'Rules to be observed by the sorters' were published in November 1882:

'The bags must be properly packed in the pouch.

'The net must be drawn up quickly after passing the standards.

'See that the pouch is duly detached from the arm, and that the arm returns to its upright position.

'Should a failure occur, the arm must be drawn in by the check cord.

'Should the pulley line break, the pouch should be eased down into the working position by the check cord.

'If the springs are weak or a strong wind is blowing, tie a piece of string once round the lever.'

The ground apparatus was supplemented by a warning board placed 250ft before the apparatus for the use of the TPO crew, and a black and yellow enamelled board which was illuminated by an electric hand lamp when the apparatus was to be used at night. This was for the benefit of the locomotive crew. It was sometimes mounted on the side of a small hut provided as a store for the lamps and spare pouches; the postman was instructed near its door whilst holding the lamp on the pouches.

The following is typical of the instructions for working the apparatus, indicating landmarks and working number of standards and net frames, in this instance applying to Atherstone, Warwickshire, for the North Western Night Down TPO in 1882: 'Apparatus 400yd north of station. Observe level crossing, fix on under bridge, notice side lines through station, lower and extend after passing level crossing gates. One standard, one net. Two pouches received. One pouch despatched.'

To ensure that the apparatus was maintained to the necessary tolerances the TPO Section maintained a five-man Mail Bag Apparatus Duty. Any work which wanted doing was usually passed on to the railway company, at GPO expense. The Duty was responsible for inspecting and approving all installations, both on the ground and on rolling stock. It was also the agent for testing those who worked the apparatus.

Apparatus working was not without its hazards, some already alluded to, and the men themselves thought it was especially dangerous at higher speeds. However, it was not only the postal workers who were at risk. On 19 February 1889 a woman travelling from Aberdeen put her head out of the window at Beattock and was hit by a pouch mounted on the lineside apparatus. She died in Carlisle Infirmary and her mother lost a case for negligence brought against the Caledonian Railway, it being found that the company was not at fault because the equipment was required by the GPO. Subsequent to this incident TPOs were

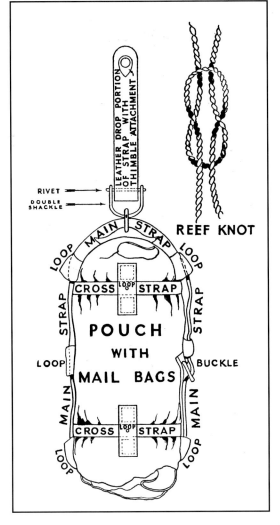

placed at the front of trains with passenger portions so any exchanges had taken place before the passengers passed protruding apparatus. This didn't always meet with the approval of the TPO staff as the ride quality deteriorated; consequently on some services a 'buffer brake' was interposed between the locomotive and TPO.

Enginemen were not immune either, for on 25 July 1936 King's Cross-based driver Alfred Peacock broke his arm when driving an Edinburgh-bound train near Hitchin. He had leaned out of his cab to look for signals and his arm was caught by the TPO apparatus. The following year, on 1 June, in a similar situation driver W. Tyler was killed at Sandy when driving the 8.25pm from King's Cross for Edinburgh.

Sometimes mishaps simply involved the pouches and their contents. In November 1885 a pouch being set down from the Midland TPO at Cudworth, near Barnsley, was damaged and the contents strewn along

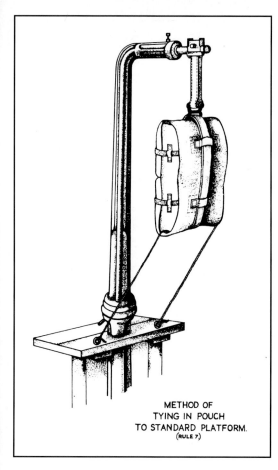

METHOD OF
TYING IN POUCH
TO STANDARD PLATFORM.
(RULE 7)

Left: **The make-up of the pouch.** *Peter Johnson Collection*

Above: **Fixing the pouch on the lineside.** *Peter Johnson Collection*

the line as far as Normanton, some 15 miles. The rule book had the answer:

'15. *Contents of mail bags scattered.* If any bag or pouch has been damaged, and the contents scattered, careful search should be made of the line for any correspondence that may have fallen out. Any items found should be taken to the local Post Office. The chalked number of the pouch, if known, should be reported. A telegram should also be sent reporting the matter to the Assistant Controller, TPO Section, London Postal Region.

'If there is any reason to believe that items have been scattered over a large area, or between the lines where it is unsafe to make a search, the Signalman should be informed and asked to obtain the assistance of plate-layers to continue the search.'

Existing accounts of apparatus working have usually been made by visitors to TPOs; whilst recognising the skill and danger involved they don't say what it was actually like to work the apparatus. One old hand the author met merely said 'it was all right up to about 80mph, but you kept well back when those things (the pouches) came flying in'. A supervisor on the Great Western TPO was recorded in *The Windsor Magazine* in 1899 as saying 'The marked improvement in the apparatus for receiving the mail bags is beyond comprehension. True, at that time (*circa* 1860) we had the nets, but they were very crude in construction. We had to lower them the best way we could, and when we caught the pouches we had to haul them into the interior of the carriage by sheer physical force. Now the operator has simply to push down a lever, a feat which does not require much exertion.'

Below: **The Up Special at Shap Wells on 30 June 1961; the carriageside lights are on ready for apparatus working.** *Derek Cross*

T.P.O. No. 75.

NORTH-WESTERN AND CALEDONIAN T.P.O.

No. of Unsorted from I.B.

Down Night Mail.

Date Stamp.

Day of the Week.

Duties.	Officers on Duty.	Officers Learning.	Stations.		Proper Time.	Sat. Night	Actual Time.	Remarks as to Delays, &c.
London to Carlisle.								
Inspector.—Charge of Mail. Tick sheet. Check London bag lists. Examination of missent bags			Euston	dep.	8 30	8 30		
Registered Letter Officer.—Charge of front end of train at stations. Enter orders and correct books			Rugby	arr.	10 8	10 11		
Clear Euston Late Fee Box (ex. Sun.) T.P.O. Late Fee Box. Watch and time bill. Sort English letters on No. 1 side to Warrington, and Scotch with No. 11 to Carlisle	1		„	dep.	10 12	10 14		
Sort English letters on No. 2 side to Warrington, Scotch to Carlisle. Make up North British bags. Assist in receipt of baskets in Aberdeen brake at Crewe. Sort London to Caledonian T.P.O. 2nd Div. letters on Saturday. Pack Glasgow letter carriage, and distribute stores for use	2		Tamworth	arr.	10 45	10 48		
			„	dep.	10 51	10 54		
			Crewe	arr.	11 49	11 54		Sunday night.
			„	dep.	12 0	12 5		11 55
Sort English letters on No. 1 side. Stirling Div. Scotch. Assist in Aberdeen parcel van at Crewe	3		Wigan	arr.		12 50		
Sort English letters on No. 2 side. Assist in Edinburgh parcel van at Crewe. Sort London to Cal. T.P.O. 2nd Div. news.	4		„	dep.		12 58		
			Preston	arr.	12 59	1 18		12 54
Open English bags, assist, sort news. Despatch news. Preston to Carlisle. Tie and seal Carlisle despatch. Transfer stores to Scotch carriage	5		„	dep.	1 5	1 21		1 0
			Carnforth	arr.	1 34	1 55		1 29
Tick off at Euston bags for Liverpool. Sort English news. Bag off No. 1 side. Assist in despatching pouches at Warrington, Lancaster, Oxenholme, and Penrith. Transfer Scotch enclosure bags. Despatch London bags for Manchester	6		„	dep.	1 38	1 59		1 33
			Carlisle	arr.	2 48	3 22		2 43
			„	dep.	2 54	3 28		
Tick off bags at Euston for 1st Glasgow carriage. Despatch Preston bags from London. Sort English news. bag off No. 2 side. Sort Irish correspondence for Stranraer route	7		Carstairs	arr.	4 18	4 55		
			„	dep.	4 24	5 7		
Pack London bags in Aberdeen carriage. Sort I.B. to Edinburgh Div. and Ayrshire Div. news. Open Scotch enclosure bags. Sort and bag off news. No. 1 side. Despatch pouches at Bletchley and Ayrshire bags at Carlisle	8		Motherwell	arr.		5 29		
			+ „	dep.		6 36		
Hang Scotch bags and English sacks. Strap bag duty. Assist No. 10 apparatus work. Pouch London bags for Warrington, Lancaster, Kendal, and Penrith. Fold empty bags for Up Special Mail. Tie and seal No. 1 side English bags. Clear Euston Late Fee Box on Sundays	9		Coatbridge	arr.		6 44		
			„	dep.		6 45		
Hang English bags. Apparatus duty. Empty bag duty. Tie and seal English bags made up on No. 2 side	10		Larbert	arr.		7 9		
			„	dep.		7 11		
Sort London to Cal. T.P.O. 1st Div. letters and No. 1 Scotch. (No. 13 on Saturday)	*11		Stirling	arr.	5 16	7 23		
			„	dep.	5 19	7 26		
Tick off London bags in 2nd Glasgow carriage. Sort London, Carlisle, and Ayr Div. letters and No. 2 Scotch. Make up Ayrshire bags and Aberdeen, Dundee, Perth, and Inverness. Sunday tick off all bags at Euston	12		Perth	arr.	5 54	8 10		
			„	dep.	5 58			
Assist to enter orders ex. Sat. Pack London bags for Carlisle, Ayrshire, and North British lines in Aberdeen brake at Euston. Sort London to Cal. T.P.O. 1st Div. news. Sort news. Bag off No. 2 side, ex. Sat. Saturday night Lond. to Cal. 1st Div. letters and No. 1 Scotch	13		Aberdeen	arr.	7 35			
Assist generally	*14							

London to Crewe.

Tick off London bags for Manchester. Stamp and divide all Late Fee and London unsorted letters. Sort London to North-Western Div. letters and news. and London to Edinburgh Div. letters. Irish miss. ltrs. Assist bag and app. duty Rugby to Nuneaton and Tamworth No. 2 despatch ...... †15

Preston to Perth.

Assist N.W. No. 1 side. Sort No. 2 Div. letters from Birmingham, Liverpool, Manchester, and Mid. T.P.O. Sth. Sort and bag off all letters received south of Carlisle (except from E.C.) for bags despatched between Stirling and Meikleour after Carlisle for all bags down to same point ... *1

Sort and bag off London to Cal. 2nd Div. letters. Open all Cal. T.P.O. bags. Sort all papers also Stirling and Carlisle Div. news. from N.W.T.P.O. and assist 2nd parcel officer despatch baskets at Stirling and Perth *2

Carlisle to Aberdeen. (Perth on Sunday.)

Overseer.—Charge of Mail, tick sheet, time bill and watch ....

Registered Letter Officer.—Transfer all bundles of empty bags for Up Special Mail to Aberdeen parcel van at Perth on Sunday mornings ....

Late Fee Box. Sort letters (except from E.C.) for Edinburgh sub-offices. Sort and despatch letters (except E.C.) for places north of Perth. Sunday morning all Cal. T.P.O. letters and those left over by North-West. T.P.O. West Highland bags in season. Search carriage 1

Assist to sort news. Bag off news. for same places as 1st Carlisle officer bags off letters. Transfer all bundles of bags for Up Special Mail to Aberdeen parcel van on week days. Tie and seal Edinburgh sub-office bags and transfer them. Assist in despatching pouches. Despatch baskets from Aberdeen brake at Stirling and Perth on Sunday morning 2

Apparatus, strap, and empty bag duty. Assist tying and sealing 3

Nos. of Watches.	Nos. of T.P.O. Carriages.
London to Aberdeen (Perth Suns.) Letter Mail	Aberdeen P.C.
	Aberdeen L.C.
Do. do. Parcel Mail Received by	Glasgow L.C. 1st „ L.C. 2nd
	‡Edinboro' P.C.
	Glasgow P.C.
Keys, Seals, and Electric Bells Intact. Signature.	Late Fee Box.
London to Carlisle	To Carlisle
Carlisle to Aberdeen (Perth Suns.)	To Aberdeen (Perth Suns.)

Officers from Inland Branch.

1.

London to Preston R.L. duty. (Not on Fri., Sat., or Sun.)

2.

3.

4.

‡ Waits for 8.50 p.m. from Euston.

* Not on Saturday.   † Not on Sunday.   ‡ Does not run on Sunday between London and Carlisle.

a (5)4093. 500.—8/98. Wt. 7407. E. & S.

Duties on the North Western and Caledonian TPOs, 1898.
C. J. Whitehead Collection

Bags. Despatched.	Bags. Despatched.	Bags. Despatched.	Bags. Despatched.	Bags. Despatched.	Bags. Despatched.
Euston.	**Crewe Stn.—** *cont.*	**Carlisle Stn.—** *cont.*	**Carstairs Junc.**	**Stirling Stn.** *—cont.*	**Stanley Junc. (App.)** *(not on Sunday).*
*I.B. Missorts	Stockport	Aberdeen	‡Auchenheath	‡Bucklyvie	Stanley
Bletchley (App.)	Stony Stratford	,, R.L. Bag	‡Arbroath	Bridge of Allan	
Bletchley	‖UpL'm'dTransfer	‡Ancrum	‡Balerno	‡Callander	**Cargill (App.)** *(not on Sunday).*
	,, R.L. Bag	Annan	‡Burnbank`	‡Cambus	‡Meikleour
Weedon (App.)	‖ Up Sp'l Transfer	Ayr	‡Carnoustie	‡Connel	
Weedon	Wolverhampton	Carlisle & AyrS.C.	Carnwath	Craignure	**Coupar Angus (App.)** *(stop on Sunday).*
	Wrexham	,, R.L. Bag	‡Carstairs Junc.	‡Crieff 1st	Coupar Angus
Rugby Stn.		cCanonbie	‡Coalburn	‡Dollar	Blairgowrie
Birmingham Ltrs	**Warrington (App.)**	Castle Douglas	Colinton‡	Drimnin	
,, R.L. Bag	Warrington	Dalbeattie	Currie	‡Gartmore Stn.	**Alyth Junc. (App.)** *(stop on Sundays).*
,, News	Widnes	Dundee	Dunfermline	‡Kippen	‡Alyth
Coventry		,, R.L. Bag	Edinburgh	Ledaig	Meigle
L.&H.T.P.O., 1st	**Preston Stn.**	‡Duns	‡Fauldhouse	Lismore	
Northampton	Liverpool Ltrs.	Dumfries	Fort William	‡Menstrie	**Forfar (App.)** *(stop on Sunday).*
Rugby	,, R.L. Bag	,, R.L. Bag	φGlasgow	Morvern	‡Glamis
	,, News.	Earlston	φGreenock	Oban	Forfar
Nuneaton (App.)	,, Missent	Edinburgh	φGreenock Fwd.	Onich	Kirriemuir
Hinckley	Ormskirk	,, R.L. Bag	φHamilton	‡Port Appin	
Nuneaton	Prescot	,, Fwd. (1)	Juniper Green	Port of Monteith	**Guthrie Junc. (App.)** *(not on Sunday).*
	St. Helens	,, (2)	‡Kirkmuirhill	Stirling	
Atherstone (App.)	Southport	,, Fwd.R.L.Bag	‡Kirknewton	‡Tillicoultry	‡Arbroath
Atherstone	Wigan	Galashiels	Lanark	‡Tullibody	‡Friockheim
	Accrington	‡Galloway S.C.	Larkhall	Crianlarich ⌐	‡Guthrie
Tamworth Station.	,, R.L. Bag	‡ ,, R.L. Bag	Lesmahagow	Dalmally	
Bedford	Blackburn	‡Gatehouse	Midcalder	Doune	**Bridge of Dun (App.)** *(stop on Sunday).*
Burton-on-Trent	Blackpool	Glasgow	φMotherwell	‡Killin	Brechin
Derby	Burnley	,, R.L. Bag	‡Netherburn	Lochawe	
‖Huddersfield	Chorley	‡Greenlaw	Newmains	Lochearn-	**Dubton (App.)** *(stop on Sunday).*
Hull S.T.	Clitheroe	Hawick	φPaisley	head	Montrose
Kettering	Colne	Innerleithen	φPort Glasgow	Luib	
Leeds	Lancaster Packets	Inverness	‡Rath Stn.	‡Strathyre	**Laurencekirk (App.)** *(stop on Sunday).*
Leicester	Morecambe	Jedburgh	Renfrew	Taynuilt	Laurencekirk
Lichfield	Nelson	Kelso	‡Rothesay	Tyndrum	
Loughborough	‡Newton-le-Wil-	Kilmarnock	‡Shotts		**Fordoun (App.)** *(stop on Sunday).*
Luton	lows	‡Kirkcudbright	Slateford		‡Auchenblae
Market Harboro'	Preston	Kirkgunzeon	‡Stonehouse	**Dunblane (App.)**	‡Drumlithie
Mid.T.P.O.North	,, R.L. Bag	Langholm	Strathaven	Dunblane	Fordoun
,, Forward	Settle	Lochmaben	‡West Calder		
,, South	TransfertoUpDay	Melrose		**Greenloaning (App.)**	**Stonehaven (App.)** *(stop on Sunday).*
Newcastle-on-T.		*Moffat	**Carluke (App.)**	Braco	Stonehaven
Sheffield	**Garstang (App.)**	cNewcastleton	Carluke	Crieff (Sun. only)	
Shrew.&Tam.S.C.	Garstang	‡Newton Stewart		Muthill ,,	**Aberdeen Stn.**
Stafford		Newton St. Bos-	**Wishaw (App.)**		Aberdeen
Tamworth	**Lancaster (App.)**	wells	‡Newmains	**Blackford (App.)**	,, Missent
‖Trans. to Up Ltd.	Lancaster	Peebles	Wishaw	Blackford	‡Aboyne
Wellingborough		Perth			‡Ballater
	Carnforth Stn.	,, R.L. Bag	**Motherwell** *(Sundays only).*	**Crieff Junc.** *(not Sunday).*	Balmoral (during Queen's visit)
Lichfield (App.)	Ambleside	‡Roxburgh	Glasgow	‡Comrie	‡Banchory
L.&H.T.P.O.,2nd	Barrow-in-F.	Selkirk	Greenock	‡Crieff	‡Braemar
	Carnforth	‡Stranraer	,, Forward	‡Machany	‡Dinnet
Crewe Stn.	,, R.L. Bag	Thornhill	Hamilton	Muthill	Drumoak
Altrincham	,, Missent	*Walkerburn	Motherwell	‡St. Fillans	Ellon
Ban. & Crewe T.P.O.	Kirkby Lonsdale	‡Belfast	Paisley		Fraserburgh
Birkenhead	Keswick	‡Dublin	Port Glasgow	**Auchterarder (App.)**	‡Gt. North of Scot. No. 1
Bolton	Windermere	‡Gall. S.C. Irish		Auchterarder	‡ ,, R.L. Bag
B.S. & N. East	¶Cockermouth	Cal.T.P.O.R.L. 1	**Mossend (App.)**		No. 2
,, West	¶Workington	,, ,, 2	Mossend (Sun-	**Dunning (App.)**	‡Inverurie
,, Enc.		‡ 1st Div.Lon.	days only)	‡Dunning	‡Lonmay
Bury	**Oxenholme (App.)**	‡ 2ndDiv.Lon.			‡Mintlaw Station
Buxton	Kendal	‡ (Liverpool)	**Coatbridge (App.)** *(stop on Sunday).*	**Forgandenny (App.)**	‡Peterculter
*Cardiff		‡ (Manch'st'r)	Airdrie	Forgandenny	Peterhead
Chester	**Low Gill (App.)**	‡ (Birming'm)	‡Bathgate		Strichen
Congleton	Sedbergh	‡ (do.) Fwd.	Coatbridge	**Perth Stn.**	Boddam
Crewe			‡Slamannan	Aberfeldy	Hatton Combined Mail
Dublin and Queenstown	**Tebay (App.)**	**Ecclefechan (App.)**	Mossend (except Sunday)	Ballinluig	‡KincardineO'Neil
R.P.O. Wed. only	Kirkby Stephen	Ecclefechan	‡Holytown	Banff	‡Lismahanan
Farnworth	Newbiggin			Birnam	Port Errol
Hereford		**Lockerbie (App.)**	**Larbert (App.)** *(stop on Sundays).*	‡Carnoustie	Torphins
‡Huddersfield	**Shap (App.)**	Lockerbie	‡Bonnybridge	Dundee	
Knutsford	Shap		‡Carron	Dunkeld	
L.&H.T.P.O.,3rd		**†Beattock (App.)**	Denny	Elgin	
Llandudno	**Penrith (App.)**	‡Moffat	Falkirk	‡Errol	
Macclesfield	§Appleby		Grangemouth	Highland S.C. 1	
Manchester	Penrith	**Abington (App.)**	Larbert	,, 2	
,, R.L. Bag		Abington		,, 3	
Newcastle (Staff.)	**Carlisle Stn.**		**Stirling Stn.**	,, 4	
Newport Pagnel	*Armathwaite	**Lamington (App.)**		,, R.L.Bag	
Northwich	*Appleby	Lamington	‡Aberfoyle	‡Huntly	
¶Newton-le-Wil- lows	Carlisle		Alloa	‡Inchture	
Oldham	,, N.D.S.O.	**Symington (App.)**	‡Alva	Inverness	
Oxford	,, Missent	Biggar	‡Ardgour	‡Keith	
Ruabon	‡Cockermouth	‡Stobo	‡Aros	Murtlly	
Runcorn	Harrington		‡Ballachulish	Perth	
Stoke-on-Trent	Kirkoswald	**Thankerton (App.)**	‡Bannockburn	,, Missent	
	Longwathby	Thankerton		Pitlochry	
	Lazonby			‡Turriff	
	Maryport				
	‡Wigton				
	‡Workington				

* Not on Sunday.   † Saturday Night only.   ‡ Not on Saturday Night.   ¶ Left here on Saturday and eve of Good Friday and Christmas Day.
‖ Left at Tamworth when Mail is over 20 minutes late.   § Sunday Night only.   φ Motherwell on Saturday Night.   c Combined Mail.

Made up from 31 June to 30 Sept.

Bags dispatched from the North Western and Caledonian TPOs, 1898.
C. J. Whitehead Collection

95

T.P.O. Bags Received.

Bags.	Bills.	Received.	Bags.	Bills.	Received.	Bags.	Bills.	Received.	Bags.	Bills.	Received.	Bags.	Bills.	Received.

Euston.
§Official Bag
§Gt. Westn. T.P.O.
§L. & H. T.P.O.
§S.E. T.P.O. Nws.
*I.B. Cal. 1st Div.
* „ Edin. Div.
* „ C. & A. Div.
„ N.W. T.P.O.
§ „ „ 1st Div.
§ „ „ 2nd Div.
„ „ unsorted
„ Scotch „
*¶E. D.O.
*¶N. D.O.
*¶ „ Scotch Enc.
*N.W. D.O.
* „ „ Scotch Enc.
*¶ Paddington
*¶ „ Scotch Enc.
*¶S.E. D.O.
*S.W. D.O.
* „ Scotch Enc.
*¶ W. D.O.
*¶ „ Scotch Enc.
*¶ W.C. D.O.
*¶ „ Scotch Enc.
House of Commons when sitting, ex. Sun., Wed., and Sat.
*¶Aldershot
*¶Barnet
* „ New
*¶Bournemouth
*¶Guildford
*¶Margate
*Newbury
*¶Portsmouth
*¶Ramsgate
*Reading
* „ Scotch Enc
*¶Salisbury
*¶Southampton
*¶ „ Scotch Enc
*Southampton Oxford Street
*¶Tunbridge Wells
*¶Weybridge
*¶Winchester

Harrow (App.)
§Edgware
Harrow
§ „ Weald
Stanmore
Wealdstone

Watford (App.)
Elstree
Rickmansworth
St. Albans
Watford

King's Langley (App.)
*Abbots Langley
Kings „

Boxmoor (App.)
Hemel Hempstead

Berkhamsted (App.)
Amersham
Ashley Green
Berkhamsted
Chesham

Tring (App.)
§Aylesbury
Tring

*Cheddington **(App.)**
*Aylesbury

Leighton Buzzard (App.)
Dunstable
Leighton Buzzard
Luton

Bletchley (App.)
†Abingdon
Ampthill
†Banbury
Bedford
† „ Scotch
Bicester
Bletchley
„ Scotch
Brackley
Buckingham
Cambridge
† „ Scotch
*Hitchin
†Huntingdon
*Newmarket
†Oxford
† „ Scotch
*St. Ives
†St. Neots
Winslow

Wolverton (App.)
*Castlethorpe
Newport Pagnel
*Stantonbury
Stony Stratford
Wolverton

Blisworth (App.)
*Blisworth
Towcester

*¶ **Weedon (App.)**
Daventry
Weedon

Rugby.
‡*Abingdon
‡Banbury
‡Bedford Scotch
‡Birmingham 1st
* „ Scotch Enc.
‡Bletchley 1st Nws
‡Cambridge(News)
‡ „ Scotch
*Coventry 1st
‡ „ Scotch Enc.
*Downham
‡Ely
*Gt. Yarmouth
‡*Huntingdon
*¶Kettering (Ply.)
„ Scotch Enc.
§L. & H. Day Up
§ „ Scotch
*Lowestoft
Lutterworth
*Lynn
* „ Scotch Enc.
Mkt. Harboro'
Northampton
„ Scotch
*Norwich
* „ Scotch Enc.
Oundle
‡Oxford
‡ „ Scotch
*Peterboro'
„ Scotch Enc.
Rugby
„ Scotch
‡*St. Neots
*Sharnbrook
Stamford
*Thetford
Wansford
*Wisbech
*¶Wellingboro' (Prelmy.)

Nuneaton (App.)
Hinckley
Leicester
*Loughboro'
Melton Mowbray
Nuneaton
Oakham
Uppingham

Atherstone (App.)
Atherstone

Tamworth.
Ashby-de-la-Zouch
Birmingham 2nd
„ Warr. Fwd.
„ Scotch
Burton-on-Trent
„ Scotch
Derby
„ Scotch
Grimsby S.T.
„ Scotch Enc.
Lincoln S.T.
„ Scotch
Mid.T.P.O. South
„ „ Fwd.
„ Scotch
Nottingham
„ Scotch Enc.
P. & B. S.C.
„ Scotch (occasionally)
Tamworth

Lichfield (App.)
Lichfield

Crewe.
*Altrincham
Ban. & Crewe T.P.O.
„ Scotch
Birkenhead
„ Scotch
Birmingham 3rd
B'ham. & C. S.T.
„ Scotch
B., S., & N., West
„ Scotch
*B. & P. T.P.O. Scotch.
Buxton
*Cardiff
* „ Scotch Enc.
Chester
„ Scotch
Congleton
Coventry 2nd
„ Scotch
Crewe
„ Scotch Enc.
*Dublin Scotch
*Guernsey
*Jersey
*Hereford
Knutsford
Llandudno
Macclesfield
„ Scotch Enc.
Manchester 1st Scotch
Middlewich
Newcastle(Staffs.)
*Newport (Mon.)
* „ Scotch Enc
Newtown (Mont.)
„ Scotch Enc.
Northwich
Oswestry
*Plymouth
Sandbach

Crewe—*cont.*
Shrewsbury
„ Scotch
*Shrew. & Ab.S.T.
„ Scotch
*Shrew.&HereS.T.
„ Scotch
Shrew.&Tam.S.T.
„ Scotch
Stafford
„ Scotch
Stalybridge
Stockport
„ Scotch
Stoke-on-Trent
„ Scotch
*Swansea
* „ Scotch Enc.
Winsford
Wolverhampton
„ Scotch
Wrexham

Warrington (App.)
Chorley
*Ormskirk
Runcorn
Transfer NightUp
Warrington 1st
„ Scotch Enc.
*Widnes

Wigan (*Sat. only*).
See Preston.

Preston.
Bolton
Huddersfield
„ Scotch
*Leeds 1st
* „ Sch.Enc.
Liverpool
„ Scotch
Manchester 2
„ Scotch
§Ormskirk
Prescot
Rochdale
St. Helens
*Warrington 2
* „ Scotch
Wigan
„ Scotch
Up Special T.P.O.
Preston
„ Scotch

Received at Wigan on Sat.

Lancaster (App.)
Lancaster
„ Scotch Enc.

Carnforth.
Bradford Scotch
Carnforth
„ Scotch
Hull S.T. Scotch
Leeds 2nd Scotch
Mid.T.P.O. North Scotch
Normanton
„ Scotch
*Sheffield Scotch
Wakefield Scotch
York Scotch

Oxenholme.
Kendal
„ Scotch Enc.
‖Penrith
„ Scotch Enc.
‖Up Day Mail

Carlisle.
*Aberdeen
Birmingham
Carlisle
Dumfries
I.B. Cal. 2nd Div.
Liverpool
Manchester
Mid. T.P.O. So.
*Newcastle-on-T.
*N.W.T.P.O.Trans.
Stirling
*Perth
Car and Ayr S T.
Sunday only

Summit.
Edin. & Car. S.C.
Glas. & Car. S.C.

Abington (App.)
Abington

Symington (App.)
Biggar

Carstairs Junc.
Lanark

Larbert (App.)
(Stop Sundays)
‡Edin.& New. S.T.
‡Falkirk
Larbert

Stirling.
Edinburgh
‡ „ Fwd.
Glasgow
‡ „ Fwd.
‡*Perth 1st,
Stirling

Dunblane (App.)
Dunblane

Auchterarder (App.)
Auchterarder

Dunning (App.)
‡Dunning

Perth.
‡Dundee
*‡*Forres
*‡*Inverness
φ‡*Middlesbrough
φ‡*Nairn
φ‡*Newcastle-on-T.
φ‡*York
φ‡Perth

Alyth Junc. (App.)
§Meigle

Forfar (App.)
‡Forfar

Dubton Junc. (App.)
§Montrose

Fordoun (App.)
‡Fordoun

Stonehaven (App.)
‡Stonehaven

Bags received by the North Western and Caledonian TPOs, 1898.
C. J. Whitehead Collection

Above: **Penrith, 8 September 1971. The last pick-up was made here by the Up Special on 1 October 1971.** *Post Office Newsroom*

Right: **Penrith, 8 September 1971. The last set-down was made here from the North Western TPO (Night Down) on 3 October 1971.** *Post Office Newsroom*

Left: **A TPO letter box from the inside of No 80329 on 5 September 1985.**
Peter Johnson

Below: **A railway letter handed in at Oyne on the Great North of Scotland Railway and posted on to the Aberdeen & Elgin Sorting Carriage on 15 February 1906.**
C. J. Whitehead Collection

5. TPO Postmarks, the Late Fee and Collectables

The study of the postmarks, and other instructional or informative markings applied to posted items, probably followed closely behind the interest taken in stamps shortly after the Penny Black was introduced in 1840. Certainly by the time J. G. Hendy wrote his monumental *History of the Travelling Post Offices* in 1905 he thought enough of this aspect to include detailed information on the various types of markings used on the early services. He was well placed to do this, being the curator of the General Post Office's Record Room. The late Norman Hill built on Hendy's work by producing *TPO Postmarks of the British Isles* in 1962, listing and illustrating every TPO postmark he was aware of at that time. Hill's was really a labour of love as each of the 250 pages was hand-duplicated, the technology limiting the book to a run of less than 300 copies; copies appearing in auctions have attracted bids of more than £50.00. Stubbs & Roberts brought Hill's work up to date in 1990, listing and illustrating nearly 2,000 further datestamps in *TPO Postmarks of Great Britain 1962-1990*; they have issued updates subsequently. Details of these books are given in the bibliography.

The Post Office Archives (at Mount Pleasant, London EC1A 1BB) are probably the largest single source of information for anyone interested in the TPOs. In addition to the usual business records, the archives contain the Impression Books, their pages bearing impressions of nearly every postal marking ever issued. Unfortunately there are gaps in the collection but many TPO strikes are recorded, some being otherwise unknown.

The other major source of information relating to TPO postmarks lies in items which have passed through the postal system and subsequently come into the hands of collectors. Fortunately most collectors are gregarious in nature and readily share information at their disposal.

The use of postmarks to show the origins of a postal item originated in London in 1661 and gradually spread until their usage was common throughout the country. The first travelling post offices were not issued with their own datestamps because it was not then intended that they should receive loose mail from the public. There was a need, however, to show why a letter was delayed through mis-sorting, ie being sent to a TPO in error. Therefore the first markings associated with TPOs were not concerned with the place of posting but to provide information.

The experimental TPO of 1838 was soon issued with a stamp which read, 'Missent to Railway Post Office'. As the network expanded there were stamps reading 'Missent to London & Birmingham Railway Office' and 'Missent to G.N.(Grand Northern) Railway Post Office Day'. Less informative stamps containing initials, such as 'EGW' (evening, Great Western) or 'IRPOM' (Irish, Railway Post Office, morning), served the same purpose. The earliest types contain their message in straight lines without borders; later ones were shaped as stars, lozenges or circles. In contrast, the Bristol & Exeter RPO had its own distinctive circular wax seal, now in the National Postal Museum.

The first circular datestamps were issued in the late 1860s/early 1870s. With few exceptions the name of the TPO was placed around the edge, within a border. The date was placed in the centre of the stamp, usually in two straight lines. They were mostly $^{13}/_{16}$in or $^{15}/_{16}$in diameter. The space above the date was often used to show the time or, by using letters or numerals, to show operational data. This could be an indication to show if the datestamp was being used on a day or a night mail, or an up or a down duty, or to show which crew was using it. A few of the smaller sorting carriages were issued with circular stamps which had no dates. In these instances the name of the service was placed across the centre.

From 1860 the public were allowed, subject to payment of a supplementary fee, to post letters on the TPOs; the supplement was called the late fee and it

POST CARD

THIS SPACE MAY BE USED
FOR COMMUNICATION
FOR INLAND POSTAGE ONLY.
(Post Office Regulation.)

THE ADDRESS ONLY TO BE
WRITTEN HERE

was prepaid by means of postage stamps affixed to the letter. Items posted without the late fee were held back and forwarded by the normal service. In 1891 it was decided to accept such items, with a surcharge of double the deficiency being levied on the recipient.

Boxed rectangular surcharge marks reading 'Posted without late fee 1d to pay' on two lines were issued. These tended to vary in size but the usual dimensions were about 2in by ⅜in.

A new type of datestamp was introduced from the 1890s. The outer diameter was 1in, the layout as before but the name was separated from the date by an inner ring, ⅝in in diameter. For services with a short name the space was filled with one or two thick arcs at the base. Collectors know these as 'double ring datestamps with thick arcs'. This issue was replaced from the 1950s by similar stamps having thin arcs where necessary.

A new type of tax mark also commenced in the 1950s. These measured 1⅛in by ¾in and read '1d to pay posted in TPO late fee not paid'. Each TPO had its own issue showing its PO number, a feature of some of the older types. In 1970 the surcharge marks were replaced again. The new issue was the same size but read '—d more to pay late fee unpaid', allowing the amount due to be inserted by hand. The PO number was not shown, allowing bulk production. They had a short life, being replaced after decimalisation in 1971 by an issue which indicated the new currency.

In March 1977, following the abolition of the late fee the previous September, the TPOs were issued with a tax stamp which read simply '__p more to pay'. This is for use on underpaid mail and is the same size as previous issues.

Since 1970 many services have been issued with single-ring datestamps. They were for use on

documents relating to the Datapost service and should not have been used to cancel stamps, although such use did sometimes occur; they are now obsolete. With the introduction of the new services from the late 1980s a policy of standardisation of the layout and style of datestamps was brought in, producing modified TPO titles, too. In particular anachronistic references to 'night' TPOs were removed and side numbers, see later, eventually settled down to be styled as 'No 1' or 'No 2' as appropriate. It was this programme of datestamp standardisation which resulted in the North Eastern TPO Night Up becoming the North East TPO Up from 30 May 1995, for example. The effect of this programme has been to leave only the Midland and Great Western TPOs retaining a pre-Nationalisation, or even pre-Grouping, railway company name.

Two further matters relating to the datestamps are worthy of comment. The first is that although many services run throughout the night the date is not changed at midnight for administrative reasons. As a result an interesting situation was created for collectors when new stamps were issued. It was possible to buy the new issues at midnight at the 24hr post offices at King Edward Buildings (London Chief Office) and Trafalgar Square. The stamps were affixed to first day covers and posted on to Up TPOs which arrived at London sufficiently late for those collectors who hurried to reach them at the penultimate station on their route. The result was a first day cover dated the day before the stamps were issued. In 1953 the GPO took steps to eliminate this anomaly. On the nights when new stamps were issued, the TPOs concerned were issued with a reserve datestamp bearing the correct date but with the letters AM above it; this was to allow a distinction to be made with the following night's mail which would be cancelled with the same date. The outcome was an even more desirable item for collectors!

By 1962 this applied to the Up Special, at Rugby; the East Anglian Up, at Romford; the East Anglian Up (Peterborough Section) at Bury St Edmunds; the East Anglian Down (Peterborough Section) at Ely; the Great Western Up at Reading; the South Western Up, at Surbiton; the South Eastern Up, at Croydon; and the North Eastern Up, at Peterborough. The development of the motorway system allowed trains to be reached at even greater distances. AM postmarks could be obtained on the North Western Down and the Huddersfield-Whitehaven TPOs by travelling to Preston and getting there before 03.30 — one collector hired an 'E'-type Jaguar for the purpose! In 1963 the Forth Road Bridge stamps were placed on sale at midnight in Edinburgh, creating opportunities for AM datestamps in Scotland for just the one occasion.

Disruption of railway services was closely monitored by TPO collectors in case it had an effect on TPO services when new issues were due, for the regular AM datestamp could then be in the wrong place, requiring alternative arrangements to be made, which could produce a rarity! The use of AM datestamps came to an end when the Trafalgar Square office ceased to open all night in 1981.

The second matter for comment concerning datestamps relates to side numbers, to which a passing reference has already been made. On the longer trips a crew will make a down journey the first night and return with the up on the second night. A second crew will be working in the opposite direction. To distinguish them the first will be called side 1; the second side 2. These distinctions are shown on the datestamps, so it is possible to post on the same train two nights running and get different postmarks. There were some variations to this — the Huddersfield-Whitehaven was Side 1, the Whitehaven-Huddersfield Side 2, yet this was an out and back trip worked by the same crew. On the North Western and the South Western TPOs it was also possible to get different postmarks at different ends of the trains, for example,

Left: **District Sorting Carriage marks.** *Peter Johnson Collection*

Below: **Strikes from a selection of old datestamps kept at TPO Section before being handed over to the National Postal Museum.** *Peter Johnson Collection*

Right: **A last night cover from the Peterborough Section of the East Anglian TPO.** *Peter Johnson Collection*

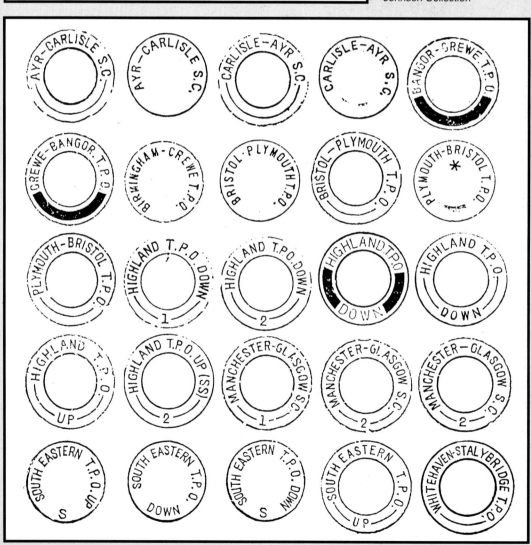

FINAL RUN

EAST ANGLIAN T.P.O.
(PETERBOROUGH SECTION)

11 May 1990

with a 2 or a 2a. The side numbers were shown in several different ways, a digit above the date, between arcs at the base of the datestamp or as 'No 1 side'; as mentioned, they are now being standardised as 'No 1' etc.

There used to be other datestamp oddities, too. For example, Edinburgh-based crews took over the London-York-Edinburgh and North Eastern Down TPOs at Newcastle using datestamps without side numbers, but with the letter E above the date. The Up Special datestamp with an L above the date was used by the crew which worked the previous night's North Western Night Down TPO, another example of different datestamps being used on different parts of the same train. These particular varieties were in regular use for many years, but for some reason were seen as difficult to get and were less often obtained by collectors.

Letters can be posted on all TPOs but collectors and enthusiasts should take care not to intrude upon, or delay, the operational function of a TPO. The public are not permitted to enter TPOs and photography on TPOs is not permitted.

There is a knack to the art of striking good datestamp impressions; quality may be improved if the train is not moving. When railway related postage stamps were released dealers would post on to TPOs for their distinctive datestamps and expect good impressions on several hundred covers — these were usually forwarded to the TPO Section for franking. Eventually this was seen as a misuse of resources and from May 1994 bulk, more than 10 items, philatelic postings on TPOs were disallowed. From that time the 'Travelling Post Office Section London' datestamp was made available, by means of a reposting service, for large, and other, postings requiring a TPO related postmark; at the time of writing the datestamp is available on any Monday-Friday date, except public holidays. Collectors wanting the datestamp on first day covers of new issues should send them on the day of issue requesting the first day date for handstamp No 3322. The address to send them to is: The Philatelic Officer, TPO Section, Royal Mail Letters, Mount Pleasant, London EC1A 1BB.

Collectors posting on TPOs should hand in any philatelic mail as early as possible so that the crew stands a reasonable chance of cancelling the stamps before departure. Affixing more than one stamp to a cover is a method of getting more than one strike, one of which may be legible!

Good strikes of older TPO datestamps and markings are scarce and attract good prices. Impressions can be found cancelling loose stamps which are still collectable. For postwar items the strikes must be clearly legible. The scarcest modern postmarks are those of the Chester Relief Sorting Carriage, followed by the temporary TPOs and first/last days of new/withdrawn services.

The previous paragraphs have concentrated on the effects of TPO operations so far as collectors are concerned. To complete the story the following are extracted from the 1955 *Rules for Officers of Travelling Post Offices*:

'Late Fee

'1.   The Late Fee box should be opened as soon as the staff attend for duty and at each stopping station *en route*. The box should be examined and the hood closed as soon as the train leaves each station.

'2.   Correspondence must be received in normal course to secure a particular postmark. Correspondence coming to hand other than in normal course, eg, received under cover by post from philatelists, should not be date-stamped but should be submitted with a covering report to the Chief Superintendent, TPO Section. Letters tendered by an agent of the sender, eg, by a Railway servant, may be accepted as if posted by the sender.

'3.   The Late Fee payable on unregistered correspondence of all classes is ½d; that for registered items is 6d.

'4.   Ordinary letters, ie, other than those referred to in 7 below, posted in the Late-Fee box without a Late Fee must be charged a double Late Fee (1d) and stamped 'Posted without Late Fee' or 'Late Fee unpaid' They must, in addition, be charged double any deficiency in ordinary postage.

'8.   Late Fee letters — whether large or small — posted in the TPO box or collected into the TPO from a station Late Fee box should be despatched by the letter officers. The large packets must not be sorted at the Newspaper Desk. The officer who stamps and divides the Late Fee letters should hand them to the respective letter despatching officers for direct disposal.

'9.   When two or more sorting carriages form the TPO only one Late Fee box should be used. '

In addition to the operational datestamps special commemorative cancellations relating to TPOs are used from time to time, although, as yet, none has actually been used on a TPO. Also to be found are commemorative covers relating to the TPOs, sometimes produced by dealers, by philatelic societies or by TPO personnel themselves; the latter

have been responsible for sets of covers recording TPO changes since 1988. Post Office-produced covers for the special events featuring TPOs are attractive items and, because they were issued in limited numbers and not to collectors, are not easy to come by; at auction they can sometimes fetch as much as £20.00; it is also worthwhile looking out for such items as the menus and other souvenirs produced for these events, for it is likely that very few of them have been collected.

A number of picture postcards featuring or relating to TPOs have been published; collecting them makes an interesting sideline. Some of those dating to the Edwardian period are quite scarce and command a good price. In more recent times several Post Office regions issued TPO postcards which proved popular and consequently are still fairly easily found.

Non-philatelic collections can also be formed. Many will know of the famous Hornby TPO model, complete with working apparatus. The older ones had tin-plate bodies but recent ones have been of plastic. Based on an LMS prototype it has even appeared in Great Western livery and still remains a popular model, even when in really incongruous combinations, such as the recent red and yellow livery with working apparatus! The Post Office actually led the way in this respect, when it commissioned a quantity of the models to be painted in the red and yellow livery to be given to guests at a publicity event. In the 1980s Lima also produced a range of TPO carriages, based on the BR designs.

Above left: **A first night cover of the North East TPO.** *Peter Johnson Collection*

Below left: **The old North Eastern TPO datestamps had 'Eastern' abbreviated.** *Peter Johnson Collection*

Top: **A first day cover for the Chester Relief Sorting Carriage.** *Peter Johnson Collection*

Above: **A surcharged cover with the late fee unpaid and the Midland TPO's AM datestamp used on stamps which were not new issues.** *Peter Johnson Collection*

Right: **The Hornby TPO model as privately customised with the red and yellow livery for the Royal Mail in 1986. Hornby later produced the model with this livery for sale, distinguishable by having the body made of red coloured plastic.** *Peter Johnson*

6. The Gentlemen of the TPOs

The *Literary World* of 1839 described the TPO as being staffed by two sorters and a mail guard, the latter for handling the bags and working the apparatus. The idea of having a mail guard was a carryover from the road mail coach and some of these men, made redundant by the TPO, were to work out their time as examiners of apparatus. The first TPO sorters were loaned from the GPO in London. The administration of the TPOs was picked up by the GPO's Mail Coach Office; in 1838 George Louis was the Surveyor & Superintendent of Mail Coaches and he arranged for the staffing of the experimental TPO. The TPO became a permanent establishment within the Mail Coach Office in 1838 and by the end of that year 10 TPO sorters, then designated railway clerks, had been appointed. It appears that day-to-day control of the TPOs was devolved to the senior railway clerk, at that time Lachlan MacLean.

In 1852 the post of Superintendent Senior Clerk was established, responsible for the TPOs under the direction of the Surveyor & Superintendent of Mail Coaches. The first holder of the new post, until 1855, was Arthur Benthall, an outsider. He was succeeded by John Churchill (1855/8) and John Willdey (1858/9) were both from the ranks of the railway clerks.

The Mail Coach Office continued in existence, by then primarily concerned with the carriage of mail by rail, until 1854, when it was replaced by the Mail Office. In 1860 the TPOs were placed under the supervision of the Inspector-General of Mails, E J. Page. In 1867 the Mail Office was divided into two parts, the Railway Post Office and the Stationary Branch. The post of Surveyor of TPOs was established, John West being appointed to it. West had become a railway clerk in November 1838 and had been Page's deputy. In turn Lachlan MacLean became West's deputy.

By 1869 West and MacLean headed an establishment of four superintendents, nine first class travelling clerks, with supervisory and inspectorial duties, 44 travelling clerks, three apparatus examiners, 151 travelling sorters and a mail porter at Euston station. The travelling clerks replaced the original railway clerks.

West became postmaster of West Central District in 1879, after 41 years on TPOs, and his departure prompted a reorganisation, the TPO branch being amalgamated with the (mail) Circulation Department. The post of surveyor was abolished and the TPOs were jointly managed by two superintendents, one responsible for the TPOs on the LNWR and the Caledonian plus those to Normanton, the other responsible for TPOs on the GWR, Midland Railway, LSWR and South Eastern Railway. In 1880 these posts were held by J. A. Duesbury and J. Huddart, the latter becoming sole superintendent following the former's retirement in 1881; the *status quo* was restored by the appointment of W. M. Brown in 1882.

Until 1882 TPOs had been part of the GPO's headquarters establishment, but the creation of the London Postal Service that year saw the TPOs transferred to it, the majority of TPO operation being undertaken by London-based personnel. Huddart became the first Chief Superintendent TPOs under the new regime.

The structure thus established remained in existence for more than 100 years, with only the Sorting Carriages not being the responsibility of the London Postal Service. As previously noted, local postmasters were responsible for Sorting Carriages, an arrangement which continued until the 1930s. To put this into context, by 1900 provincial postmasters controlled only 40 of about 240 travelling staff.

Huddart retired in 1884. Until World War 1 his successors as Chief Superintendent were J. W. Curford from 1886 until 1892 (on promotion to Assistant Controller in the LPS); F. McDonnell from 1892 until 1896 (died in office); John Edward Thomas O'Moore Carew from 1896 until 1904 (he had started on TPOs as a travelling clerk in 1866; he moved on to be postmaster of the South Eastern District Office); and H. Filmer (from 1904 until 1915, also to succeed Carew at South Eastern District Office). As Chief Superintendent TPOs Filmer's salary was £650 — John West had received £675 as Surveyor of TPOs in 1869!

Above left: **Divisional Chief Inspector Dick Escudier checks Carlisle-Street sorting on the North Western TPO (Night Down) on 20 January 1988.** *Peter Johnson*

Below left: **Loading the Midland TPO at Cheltenham on 23 March 1995.** *Peter Johnson*

The prewar years saw the TPOs reach their peak, with many services, day mails and parcel sorting especially, not being restored afterwards. Probably because of the war the Chief Superintendent's post was not immediately filled when Filmer moved on in 1915. The Principal Clerk in the Controller's Office, J. Elder, was appointed in 1917 and had probably been covering the post for some time previously; he remained in office until retirement in 1921.

Elder was replaced by William C. Waller, Principal Clerk during Filmer's time, from 1921 until 1923; Lt Col W. T. Brain (from 1923 until 1926); G. F. Gould (from 1926 until 1927); F. W. St A. Ellis (from 1927 until 1934 — during which period responsibility for the Sorting Carriages was transferred to the London Postal Service); and J. J. C. Rowden (from 1934).

In 1937 the London Postal Service was replaced by the London Postal Region. Control of the TPOs remained with the LPR, as part of the Mails & Transport branch, with Rowden taking the title of Assistant Controller TPOs. Whilst in office he wrote the GPO's Green Paper on TPOs, and oversaw the filming of *Night Mail* and the organisation of the TPO centenary celebrations. In 1939 Rowden became Controller, Mails & Transport Branch, G. Jefferson taking charge of the TPOs with the old title of Chief Superintendent. Jefferson retired early, due to ill health, in 1945.

F. G. Fielder became Chief Superintendent TPOs in 1945 and was to oversee the postwar restoration of TPOs as well as the Nationalisation of the railways. In 1949 he was replaced by G. R. Clegg, who in turn was replaced by H. Kearney in 1952. Kearney stayed until 1957 when he was replaced by L. P. Palmer. Palmer was replaced by W. Shires in 1961. Shires was to be the last Chief Superintendent TPOs, since a reorganisation of the London Postal Region saw him being designated Manager TPOs in 1966; he retired in 1972, the longest-serving head of TPOs since West in the 1870s.

Palmer's successor was P. J. G. Baker, who remained in office until 1981. From 1976, however, he had been Assistant Manager TPO in the reorganised London Postal Region's London Central Transport & TPOs section, when 'TPO HQ' became known as the TPO Section, or, to TPO personnel, 'the Section'. Baker's 'demotion' appeared to have been for internal use only, for to the Post Office at large he was still known as the Manager TPOs; Baker was succeeded by F. H. W. Rhodes, who stayed in office until 1983.

Further reorganisations in 1986 and 1988 saw TPO Section emerge as part of the London Central Transport group, under Network Operations, a Royal Mail Headquarters unit. Bringing the TPOs back to Headquarters was to restore the situation which had existed prior to 1882.

Norman J. Peachell became Head of TPO in 1984. During his term in office major changes were made to the TPO network, in both 1985 and 1988. In 1985 he had a headquarters establishment of 31, a divisional team of 10 and 653 TPO staff serving on 35 TPOs. Retiring in 1989, Peachell was replaced by Alex Obradovic. The latter saw London Central Transport renamed Royal Mail Central Transport, but with functions unchanged, in 1990.

A further reorganisation took place in 1992, when the TPO Section became part of the new London Division. In 1994 Brian Quinn, an officer whose responsibilities had included the Post Office Railway since 1984, took over from Alex Obradovic as Manager TPO.

At the time of writing the Manager has a headquarters establishment of 18, with 549 working on TPOs. The most universal grade is that of PHG (Postman Higher Grade, who do the sorting), of which there are 462, followed by 29 Postmen, who sort and stow bags. Supervisory grades are JV5 and JV4 (12 each), equivalent to assistant inspector, and JV3, inspector, of which there are seven. There are also 22 reserves. In addition to London there are 14 TPO staffing offices, ranging from Penzance to Edinburgh. Postmen wishing to work on TPOs are initially transferred on trial. Ladies have been employed on TPOs in recent times, less than 10 in 1995, but they are still predominantly a male preserve.

Above: **Senior TPO officers in 1910:** (*left to right*) **H. Filmer was Chief Superintendent from 1904 to** **1915 and W.C. Waller from 1921 to 23, S. Bussell and S.T. Leverett.** *Peter Johnson Collection*

7. Railnet

When the 1988 contract between the Post Office and British Rail came up for renewal the situation was found to be complicated by the uncertainties of rail privatisation proposals. The Post Office was planning a major road/rail distribution centre at Willesden and was also interested in taking advantage of the possible opportunity to own and operate its own trains, something which would be allowed if rail privatisation went ahead but which was unclear when negotiations commenced in 1992. Accordingly an interim contract was agreed for 1993-95, to give time for the options for the future to become clearer. A 10-year contract to run from 1996 was later agreed.

In January 1993 the Post Office published a notice of intent to procure in the *Official Journal of the European Communities*, asking potential bidders to declare an interest to build between 15 and 20 dual-voltage (25kV/750DC) multiple-units with a speed

capability of 100mph. Each train would be formed from four 66ft-long vehicles, each with a payload of 40-44 tonnes, mail being carried in containers. The four-car units must be capable of multiple working with two others, and be capable of locomotive haulage at full line speed. The trains were to be available for operation from October 1995.

On 18 June 1993 bids were received from four companies: ABB Transportation, CAF of Spain, GEC Alsthom/Metro-Cammell and Siemens of Germany. On 16 December that year it was announced that an order for 16 units had that day been placed with ABB Transportation Ltd, later ABB Rail Vehicles Ltd. In a Royal Mail Press Release the vehicles were described as follows:

'Each four-car train consists of a power/motor car fitted with overhead pantograph and three trailer cars, two of which are driving units with third rail pick-up shoes so that the finished train can be driven from a cab at either end to maximise operating flexibility.

'All four axles on the power car are driven by 290kW dc traction motors governed by

Below: **The first of the Royal Mail's Railnet trains under test at Warrington in April 1995.**
Royal Mail Newsroom

microprocessor-controlled GTO thyristor traction equipment fed either from a 750V dc busbar energised directly from the third rail shoes or from the overhead supply via a 25kV transformer and rectifier unit. Units can change from ac to dc traction in motion.

'The GEC Alsthom traction package is based on that fitted to the Class 319 dual-voltage EMUs operated by Thameslink but suitably uprated and modified to meet the requirements of the high-speed limited-stop Railnet operation ensuring high reliability under the more arduous conditions at the northern end of the West Coast route from London to Scotland.

'The cabs are another first, being modular units constructed fully fitted out in parallel to the main production line and bolted into place when complete. The structure has a steel support frame complying fully with latest crash-worthiness standards, while the sleek moulded exterior in glass-reinforced resin meets Royal Mail's aesthetic requirements. The modular approach has enabled ABB to supply Royal Mail with a complete spare cab for use as an immediate replacement in the event of damage. The working cab can then be sent off for repair without affecting the availability of the train. The roomier-than-normal cabs feature full air conditioning for driver comfort.

'The new trains will be both safe and secure. There is a dual braking system, with electro-pneumatic controls for EMU operation and a graduable air brake standardised for use with locomotive hauling. In switching from EMU to loco, the EP brakes are locked on until the air brake is connected up and fully controlled from the loco cab, thus eliminating the risk of runaway.

'Other safety features include British Rail's advance warning and vigilance systems, cab-to-cab and driver-to-train communications, with links to BR's national radio network. Mail compartments are windowless and accessed through roller shutter doors which are mechanically and pneumatically secured. For added security there is no walkway between cars.'

The first unit of what is now called Class 325 was made available by ABB from its Derby works on 28 February 1995 and sent to Crewe for type testing. AC testing later took place at Warrington, whilst arrangements for dc testing were being made to take place at Strawberry Hill or Selhurst. Provisional allocation was eight trains to Selhurst, eight to Glasgow Shields, three of the latter incorporating the Scottish crown in the Royal Mail logo applied to the trains, as opposed to the English crown in the remainder. Each train will carry 180 containers, the load being 45 tonnes. Provision has been made for the units to be converted to passenger use should the Royal Mail decide to withdraw from rail transportation at a later date.

To launch the trains to the public Royal Mail Managing Director Peter Howarth named one of them after himself at Derby on 7 July 1995. The trains entered commercial service in August 1995, working

Above left: **Super GUV No 94007 in use for stowage on the Midland TPO at Derby on 2 June 1995.** *Peter Johnson*

Above: **Class 128 Driving Motor Luggage Van No 55993 in Royal Mail livery at Marylebone on 9 May 1988.** *Peter Johnson*

between Euston and Glasgow, Liverpool and Manchester. The fleet was completed in October 1995.

The Willesden depot has cost £37million and was designed by Broadway Malyan; the contractor was Tilbury Douglas. Construction started in June 1994, with completion scheduled for Easter 1995. It consists of two main halls which together cover an area of nearly 34,000 square metres. The rail hall, covering 19,540 square metres, has seven rail platforms, 288yd long, designed for loading and off-loading mail in wheeled containers without specialised lifting equipment. There is room for an eighth platform and the roof clearance is adequate for European rolling stock. The mail trains are electrically driven but will be taken to and from the rail hall by diesel shunters, for which the roof has nearly 100 smoke vents and more than 50 extractor fans to remove exhaust fumes. Additional ventilation is provided at low level in the trackbed. The roof itself is a shallow-arched barrel vault of 76yd span with one-tenth glazed for natural lighting.

The distribution hall — the main operational building — is designed to institutional standards with a gross area of 14,170 square metres and a clear height of 12yd to the underside of the steel truss rafters, which have clear spans of 41yd. It is served by 40 road vehicle stances, incorporating dock shelters and mechanised dock levellers. It has a 10,000 square metre shallow-pitched roof 17½yd above ground with 10% roof lights.

When completed, the main building will house an advanced automatic sorting and conveyor system designed to route either bags or trays of mail to the appropriate chute for its destination. It will also have, on two mezzanine levels, accommodation to provide the building's workforce with a full range of administrative and welfare facilities.

Willesden will not be working in isolation, however, and a series of satellite Royal Mail Dedicated Rail Facility sites are planned; the first, at Low Fell, Gateshead, opened on 6 March 1995. Others will be located at Filton (Bristol), Birmingham, Glasgow, Warrington, Doncaster and Tonbridge; Southampton may be added later. The satellite terminals will vary in size from a single platform, as at Low Fell, to five, at Warrington. For the Royal Mail the benefits of these sites will be greater security, reduced handling and a saving on Railtrack charges for station use, Warrington will handle the TPOs which presently call at Crewe, for example.

The Royal Mail expects that implementation of Railnet will increase the amount of long-distance mail delivered next day by 2%.

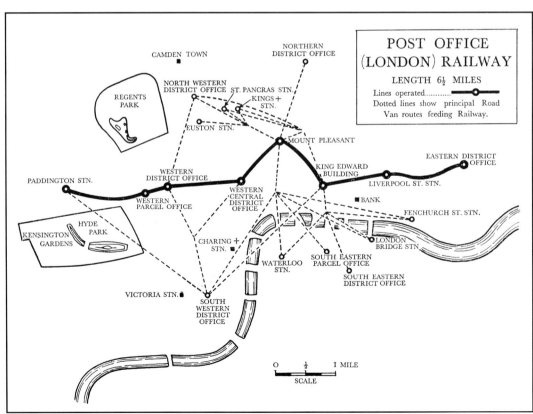

POST OFFICE
(LONDON) RAILWAY
LENGTH 6½ MILES
Lines operated............
Dotted lines show principal Road
Van routes feeding Railway.

CAMDEN TOWN

NORTHERN
DISTRICT OFFICE

REGENTS
PARK

NORTH WESTERN
DISTRICT OFFICE ST. PANCRAS STN.
KINGS +
STN.

EUSTON STN.

MOUNT PLEASANT

EASTERN DISTRICT
OFFICE

PADDINGTON STN.

WESTERN
DISTRICT OFFICE

KING EDWARD
BUILDING

LIVERPOOL ST. STN.

WESTERN
PARCEL OFFICE

WESTERN
CENTRAL
DISTRICT
OFFICE

BANK

FENCHURCH ST. STN.

KENSINGTON
GARDENS

HYDE
PARK

CHARING +
STN.

LONDON
BRIDGE STN

WATERLOO
STN.

SOUTH EASTERN
PARCEL OFFICE

VICTORIA STN.

SOUTH
WESTERN
DISTRICT
OFFICE

SOUTH EASTERN
DISTRICT OFFICE

0   ½   1 MILE
SCALE

8. The Post Office Railway (London)

Although it actually opened in 1928, the story of the Royal Mail's 2ft gauge underground railway dates back nearly 20 years previously, when in 1909 a Departmental Committee was established to discover how the transportation of mails between the principal post offices and railway stations in London could be improved, to avoid delays caused by traffic congestion and fog.

Various proposals had been made previously, primarily by would-be suppliers or contractors, and a privately-owned 2ft gauge, pneumatic tube had operated successfully over the 600yd between Euston and the GPO's Northern District Sorting Office in 1863. A second line, from Euston to Holborn, 1½ miles, was built to 3ft 8½in gauge and opened in 1865; this was extended to the London Chief Office at St Martin's le Grand and completed in 1869. Despite the success of the first pneumatic tunnel, the GPO declined to use the larger one, perhaps because the underground journey saved only four minutes compared to the overground one. A public parcels service, not covered by the GPO monopoly on letters, was offered but could not generate sufficient revenue to cover operating costs and interest on capital. In 1874 the Postmaster-General declared emphatically that the GPO had no intention of using the tunnel, forcing the company to shut up shop and wither away.

The 1909 brief was to deliberate on the relative merits, for the transmission of mails, of the various systems of pneumatic tubes and underground electric railways; the advantages and disadvantages of those systems compared with the present methods of transmitting mails; and the increase or reduction in expense which might be anticipated if any such system were established on the route or routes in London which were most suitable for the purpose.

Following investigations on the Continent and in America the committee recommended that the GPO's requirements could be met by an underground tube railway of 2ft gauge, with electrically-driven trains working in both directions, automatically and without drivers. The railway would meet three main objectives: to accelerate the transit time of mails between (sorting) offices; to even out the flow of work in the sorting offices; and to make some contribution towards relieving street congestion. The last point shows the government-department ethos coming through; although the objectives were based on conditions existing in 1909, when horse-drawn vehicles were the norm, congestion was considerably worse when the railway was eventually brought into use and motor vehicles had taken over — by 1937 it was thought that the railway carried the equivalent to 750,000 motor-van-miles.

The committee further recommended that the tunnel should be of 7ft 6in diameter, with twin tracks, except in stations, where loops would allow through running whilst loading/unloading took place. An operating headway of 1½min would provide a capacity of 40 trains per hour. The committee made recommendations regarding the nature of the rolling stock, too, proposing that self-propelled wagons would be beneficial because they would require to be neither shunted nor turned.

The first section to be built was to connect the east and west ends of London, with stations at Paddington District Office, Western Parcels Office, Western District Office, West Central District Office, Mount Pleasant, King Edward Building, Liverpool Street Station and the Eastern District Office, a distance of 6½ miles. The stations at Paddington and Liverpool Street were to connect with the respective main line stations. Journey time from Paddington to King Edward Building would be 10min, compared to 29min for a horse-drawn van travelling at 7½ miles per hour. It was further proposed that a number of extensions should be built in the light of experience with the first section, but in the event there was only ever to be the first section and the extension proposals gathered dust, never to be implemented.

Finding approval within the GPO, the railway proposals were submitted to the Cabinet, for the GPO was then a government department, and construction was finally given approval by means of an Act of Parliament which received Royal Assent on 15 August 1913. The line was to be built within five years and was not to cost more than £1 million. As a four-rail

Above left: **The Eversholt Street-Euston pneumatic tube in 1863.** *Peter Johnson Collection*

Left:
The route of the Post Office Railway as built. *Peter Johnson Collection*

113

electrical system was to be used, the tunnel diameter had been increased to 9ft.

In 1914 a contract was let for tube tunnelling, station construction and earthworks. At the same time a test track was built at Plumstead, on land belonging to the Woolwich Arsenal. At 530yd long, the test track was used to evaluate systems for electrical control, including braking and speed. Provided with curves as tight as 60ft and having gradients as steep as 1 in 20, two prototype cars built by English Electric were used on it. These cars had only detail differences from those eventually built.

The outbreak of World War 1 was responsible for the suspension of work on the electrical systems but tunnelling work was allowed to continue until completed. The empty tunnels were used as a store for artefacts from various London-based museums until 1919.

Left: **One of the 1914-prototype cars.** *Royal Mail*

Below left: **A three-car train of the four-wheel 1925 stock; with a capacity of half a ton, the cars were 13ft 5in long. One survives at Mount Pleasant.** *Royal Mail*

Below: **One of the three battery locos supplied to the Post Office Railway in 1926 and still in service. Seen at Mount Pleasant on 14 June 1995.** *Peter Johnson*

Postwar inflation caused further delay to the project, leading to a redesign of the electrical installation. Contracts were eventually let in 1924. In May 1927 half the line was made available for training purposes, the remainder being completed that December.

In brief, the railway consists of a steel-lined circular tunnel constructed at a depth of about 70ft. It is level for the greater part of the route, but deviations exist where it has had to be taken either above or below the passenger railway tubes, sewers and other services.

It has two running tracks over which trains run automatically in each direction. It is 6½ miles long, the eight stations being connected with a Post Office building, or a main line railway station.

A station actually consists of two larger parallel tunnels constructed on the same horizontal plane and joined together by cross passages. The stations vary in length, the longest being 313ft, and the shortest 90ft. Each station is raised above the level of the main line running track so that the effects of gravity mean that arriving trains are decelerated, and those departing are accelerated.

The running tunnel is circular and has an internal diameter of 9ft. It is lined with flanged steel segments, 20in wide, bolted together. Near stations the tunnel branches into two single-track tunnels of 7ft diameter and these join up to the two station tunnels, which are of 21ft 2½in or 25ft diameter. Most station layouts

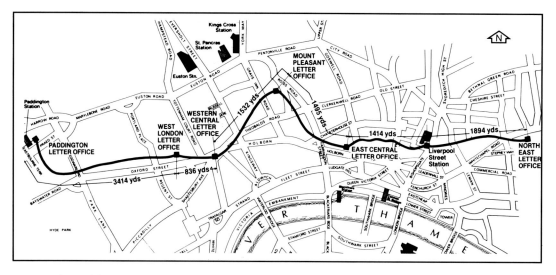

Above: **The route of the Post Office Railway, after being diverted to the West London Letter Office in 1958, showing distances between stations.** *Peter Johnson Collection*

Right: **A Post Office Railway train register used at Paddington in June 1975; the arrival of the first mails from the Great Western TPO were recorded at 02.10.** *Peter Johnson Collection*

are complex, with reversing loops as well as more straightforward sidings; at King Edward Building there is even a reversing spiral. The bottom of the mainline tunnel is filled with loose ballast covered over with a concrete raft 12in thick. Inverts are formed in this for each running track, and oak (later jarrah) sleepers are let into the concrete at intervals of 4ft 3in.

The running track consists of 35lb flat-bottomed rails. One of these rails is electrically continuous, and bonded to the tunnel and also to a bare copper conductor to provide a return path for the current. The other rail is insulated, and divided into sections for track-circuiting. The conductor rail consists of 15lb channel-sectioned mild steel and is mounted on insulators so that it lies centrally between, but 3in above, the pair of running rails. This rail is also divided into sections insulated from each other. The running rails are silicon steel; crossings and turnouts manganese steel.

Opposite each station platform there are two running tracks, one for non-stopping trains, and the other for bringing stopping trains alongside the platform. The latter track is divided along its length to provide the number of train berths, from one to three on each platform, which the station is designed to accommodate.

Electricity was originally brought to three substations on the railway at 6,600V three-phase ac; now the National Grid supplies 11,000V to five substations. The voltage is transformed and rectified, using silicon rectifiers, to dc at 440V. The 440V dc is used for driving the trains over the main line, with a maximum speed of 35mph, for starting trains, for station lighting, lifts, conveyors, and other auxiliary plant.

Current is also needed at 150V. Giving a maximum speed of 8mph, it is used by the trains when passing over low-speed sections, for operating contactors, and for working the point motors.

The track circuits are supplied with -24V dc from electronic power converters; they are used to prove the track clear, to set up certain safeguards, and finally to complete the 150V circuit used for operating the contactor switch which controls the current to the conductor rail.

When running between stations the trains are under automatic control, a dead conductor rail section always being maintained between any two trains, and so the possibilities of overtaking or collision are avoided.

Until 1993 each station had a switch cabin with a lever frame and an illuminated track diagram. On this were shown the various sections of the track in the station area and those half-way to the stations on each side. On this the switchman could follow the movement of any train in the area controlled from his station.

The platform berths are as short as possible, and it was soon found that trains were apt to stop short of, or slightly overrun, the berths due to variations of speed when arriving at the station approaches. Such variations were due to the difference in loads carried, and also to the alteration of conditions set up by trains which may have been halted in the main line tunnel, as opposed to those under which a train arrived after an uninterrupted run from the station in the rear. In order to overcome this difficulty, a camshaft apparatus was fitted at each station by means of

POST OFFICE RAILWAY.
Train Register.

PADDINGTON Station.

......Fri...... day / ......Sat...... day, the ...20th.../...21st... of ......June......, 19.45...

EASTBOUND							WESTBOUND						
Set No.	Destination	due A.M.	arrived	departed	No. of mins. late	Remarks, Special Trips, and Unscheduled Loco. Movements.	Set No.	Destination	due A.M.	arrived	departed	No. of mins. late	Remarks, Special Trips, and Unscheduled Loco. Movements.
6	LIV	2.25	2.91	2.21			6	LP	2.18	2.18	2.20		
7		30	26	30			7		23	23	24		
8		35	31	35			8		28	28	30		
9		40	36	40	21)	45	9		33	33	35	21)	38
10		45			19)	50	10		38			19)	43
11		48			17)	55	11		45			17)	48
12		51			1)	3-00	12		47			1)	53
13		54			Y Nodly								
14		58	ISL 170 68 200		2)	5	14		50			2)	58
15		3.2			Y E ody								
1		6			7)	10	1		53	ILL 400 74 126		3)	3-03
2		10			4)	15	2		58			4)	8
3		14			5)	20	3		3-3			5)	13
4		18			6)	23	4		8			6)	18
5		22			7)	27	5		13			7)	23
6		26			8)	30	6		18			8)	28
7		30	LAP - MDO		9)	35	7		23			9)	30
8		34			21)	38	8		27			21)	34
9		38					9		31			10)	38
10		42	3-40	3-42			10		35			11)	41
11		46	44	46			11		39			12)	43
12		50	45	50			12		43			14)	47
13		54		54	Y W.S.I.		13		47			1)	52
14		58	51	58			14		51			2)	57
15		4.2		4-2	X E.S.I.		15		55			3)	4-2
1		6	4-2	6			1		59			4)	4
2		10	6	10	First GWTPO		2		4-3			5)	12
3		14	10	14	E.D.O		3		7			6)	17

Signature of Switchman ...J. Woodgets.........................

BRITISH POST OFFICE SOUVENIR COVER

50th Anniversary of the Post Office Railway

Mr N H Collins
3 Fair Way Close
EASTBOURNE
East Sussex
BN20 8DB

which all trains are momentarily stopped at the station approach. They are then given a short application of 440V for a quick start and proceed into the station on 150V, at an even speed of 8mph, which ensures accurate berthing.

Opposite each train berth in the stations is a switch called the 'train ready signal'. This is used by the platform staff when the train has been loaded and secured for travelling, and is ready for dispatch. At stations where coupling or uncoupling of cars to form two-car or single car trains is carried out, switches are provided on the platforms by means of which the second car can be inched up to the leading one without any manual effort.

Battery locomotives are stationed at Paddington and Mount Pleasant. The points to their sidings are locked, operated by the king lever key, preventing the locomotive from being brought out with the conductor rail still live.

The first cars had a large centre bag compartment measuring 4ft 6in by 2ft 5in with a height of 3ft 7in, and at each end, over the motor, a smaller compartment the same shape, but only 2ft high. They were provided with containers for carrying the mail bags. There were 90 cars in all, built by English Electric, and the practice was to run them as trains in groups of three coupled together. They provided the complete service for 1928 and 1929, and part of the service for 1930 and 1931, being finally withdrawn from use in May 1931. The total mileage run at that date was 11,250,000, or an average of 125,000 miles per car. The train-mileage approximated to 1,250,000 per annum.

Above: **The philatelic cover produced to commemorate the Post Office Railway's 50th anniversary.** *Peter Johnson Collection*

Above right: **A view of the Mount Pleasant Workshops on 14 June 1995.** *Peter Johnson*

Right: **One of the 1930-units at Mount Pleasant in August 1979; this train was painted yellow.** *Peter Johnson*

The original cars were quickly found to be deficient in design and expensive to operate. They were also barely able to cope with the increasing traffic. It was clearly essential that further capacity should be provided either by increasing the number of cars or by introducing new cars designed to carry greater loads.

The old cars had a fixed wheelbase of 7ft 3in, and it was also found that this feature was responsible for rapid wear on the rails, and also on the wheels themselves. This undesirable wear naturally also increased power consumption.

Therefore new cars with a 4ft wheelbase and a centre body capable of carrying four containers, supported at each end on a motor-driven bogie, were introduced from 1930. One of the main difficulties was to keep the overall length of such a car within the required limits for negotiating tunnel curves, and also berthing in stations. To do this it was necessary to arrange for one pair of wheels of each bogie to be situated under the centre body. As this latter had to be kept at practically platform height from the rails, 15in, the largest possible diameter for such wheels was

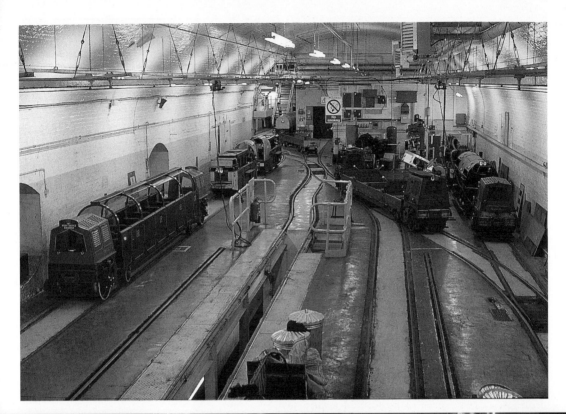

Left: **Painted the then standard GPO Engineering Department green, one of the 1930s units at Mount Pleasant in August 1979.** *Peter Johnson*

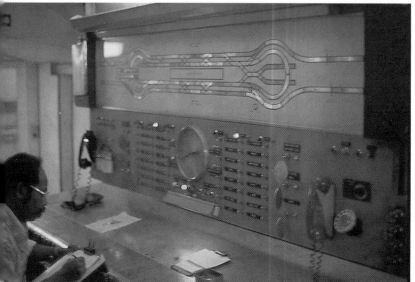

Centre left: **The original track diagram in the Mount Pleasant switch cabin, August 1979.** *Peter Johnson*

Below: **Giving the right away for one of the 1930s-built trains at Mount Pleasant, August 1979.** *Peter Johnson*

Below right: **By Spring 1987 the track diagram and control panel at Mount Pleasant had been replaced.** *Peter Johnson*

12in; they gave considerable trouble initially, for they frequently jumped the rails at sharp curves or points. Various expedients were introduced to overcome the trouble, but this was not finally done until all the old cars had been taken out of service and the new cars had had the opportunity of modifying and wearing the track in a way more suited to its requirements.

Many parts of the old cars, such as motors, driving wheels, axles and so on, were reused in the construction of the new ones, and 50 of these cars were obtained from English Electric to replace the 90 old ones. This number had a total mail-bag-carrying capacity equivalent to that of 150 of the original stock, which at the time was considered sufficient to provide a 25% margin above the maximum loads then being carried. This was soon exceeded, and in 1936 a further 10 cars were obtained from English Electric.

When the new cars took over, the whole service energy consumption was reduced by 38.5%, or £3,200 a year. The cost of renewing the track quickly fell by £1,200 a year, too, and that of the wheels by a similar amount. By the end of 1936 these cars had run over 10,500,000 miles, the average mileage per car thus being over 200,000, a considerably greater figure than that of the old ones.

The bogies at each end are identical. They are each fitted with a king pin, which registers with a hole in each end of the centre body, so permitting rotation as well as providing the means of carrying the load. The bogie consists of a steel framework shaped like a box, with an extension or tail-piece for carrying the pair of 12in pony wheels. The main weight is borne by a pair of larger driving wheels, 24in in diameter. On the axle of these wheels is fitted a gear wheel, which engages with a pinion on the electric motor used for driving the bogie. This motor is also partly suspended on the axle. There are two current collector shoes on each bogie so spaced to bridge gaps in the conductor rail. From the collector shoes the current first passes through resistances, which are provided to prevent heavy surges when current is first applied whilst the car is at rest. These resistances also act as buffers to avoid partial short-circuiting between adjacent shoes when the car passes from the 400V sections to those of 150V, or vice versa. From the resistances the path of the current is next to the brake solenoid. The plunger of this is mechanically connected to the brake rigging, and the solenoid has sufficient power, when energised, to pull the brake blocks away from the wheels, overcoming the tension of the springs which keep the brake blocks applied when no current is passing.

The next part of the bogie equipment through which the current passes is the car reverser, which can be set in any one of three positions, in accordance with the direction required. With the handle set in the intermediate position no current can be passed through the bogie equipment, and a mechanical interlock is freed, which permits the brake blocks to be screwed, so leaving the car free for pushing by hand, or for being pulled/pushed by a battery locomotive. This interlock also makes it impossible for the reverser handle to be moved from the centre position until the brakes have been restored to their normal position. From the reverser, current connections are next taken to the motor, and from there the return path is by way

of the axle and wheel to that running rail which is not used for track-circuiting.

There are three battery locomotives for rescuing faulty trains and for hauling works trains. Each loco has sufficient reserve to enable it to draw or push two-car trains along the complete length of the line at an average speed of 12mph. In 1995 two locos are stabled at Mount Pleasant, one at Paddington.

The centre of railway activity is the Car Depot at Mount Pleasant, located at a level between that of the station below and the sorting office yard above. The Depot is connected with the station tracks by two roads which rise or fall on a gradient of 1 in 20. The ascent to the depot is effected in the normal running manner, and the train comes to rest at the crest of the gradient just inside the depot. Movements in the depot are provided for by means of 150V current supplied to overhead trolley wires. A travelling carriage passes the current to the car by means of a trailing cable. The movements can be controlled either from the ground by a trailing cable or from a raised central platform by hand controllers. When being dispatched from the depot, the train is first positioned at the top of the gradient just past a scotch block, at which point it is taken over by the operational railway.

The depot is provided with inspection pits and a short length of track with a conductor rail is also provided, on which preliminary adjustments can be made to the cars after overhaul. The depot is fully

equipped with power-operated and manual machines so that all minor repairs and adjustments can be carried out on site, and it is only on rare occasions that outside assistance is required. Motor rewinds are also undertaken there.

At intervals of 10 days each car is brought into the depot for cleaning and adjustment. In addition, each car is completely stripped down at two-yearly intervals for the replacement of worn parts and any necessary reconditioning. A card index history for each car is also maintained for the recording of all faults, changes of equipment, renewal of wheels, and miles run.

Cleanliness of the station premises is ensured by frequent vacuum-cleaning of walls, passages, shafts and so on, three portable electrically-driven machines being in use continually for this purpose. A larger outfit, mounted on a suitable trolley, is taken into the main tunnel each weekend, and a section of the running track, walking paths and cables are then thoroughly cleaned. From 1984 a programme of lining the station tunnels with insulated panels was commenced, having the effect of making them warmer, brighter and saving money.

During World War 2 the Post Office Railway experienced a loss of personnel to the forces and reduced operating times due the use of stations as dormitories. During the blitz the railway was several times affected by flooding after bombing but it was not until 1943 and 1944 that the railway suffered serious damage due to enemy action. Even then the longest period of disruption was three weeks, when the Western Parcels Office was closed, its traffic diverted to road.

A quarter-mile deviation to serve the new West London Letter Office was opened in 1965, permitting the closure of the old Western District Sorting Office and the Western Parcels Office. The new station was unique for it was not of tunnel construction, being located in the sub-basement of the sorting office.

Traffic reached a peak in 1962, at the same time as two prototype cars were delivered from English Electric. Intended to be faster, they underwent several years of tests and modifications, and only one now exists. It was not until the late 1970s that it was decided that the 1930 and 1936-built cars should finally be replaced, an order for 34 cars placed with Greenwood & Batley of Leeds being announced in April 1979. Apart from the first three, the new cars were built jointly by Greenbat and the Hunslet Engine Co, also of Leeds. The first of the new stock was delivered in 1980, the last in 1982. The superseded stock was offered for sale in the railway press, resulting in Unit 809 passing to the National Railway Museum, No 807 to the Science Museum, No 803 to the Buckinghamshire Railway Centre and No 808 being acquired by the Diesel & Electric Group for display at Minehead station on the West Somerset Railway. In 1993 No 808 passed to the Chalk Pits

Above: **Ancient and modern at Mount Pleasant, Spring 1987. Both units are painted red with yellow 'buffer' beams.**
Peter Johnson

Right: **One of the Greenbat units at Paddington, showing the insulated panels fitted to the roof, photographed in December 1987.**
Peter Johnson

Lower right: **The 1994 Control Centre.** *Peter Johnson*

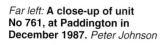

Far left: **A close-up of unit No 761, at Paddington in December 1987.** *Peter Johnson*

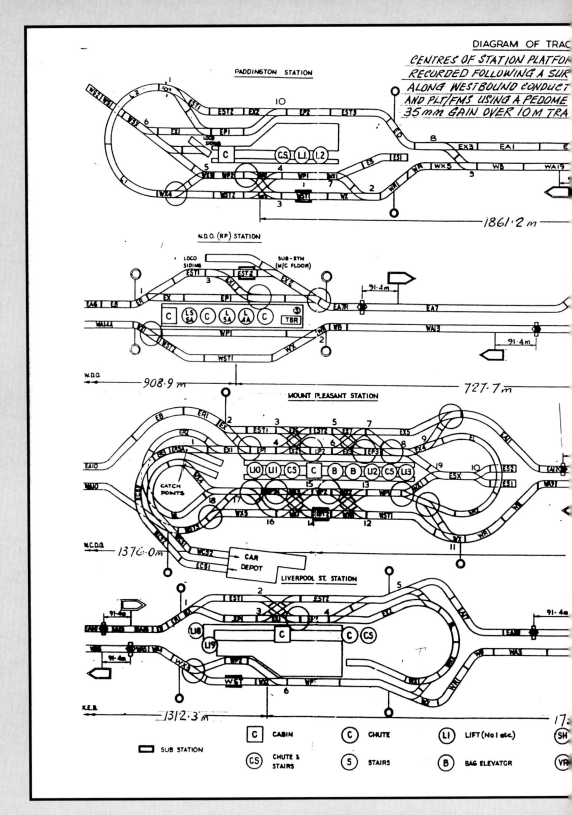

DIAGRAM OF TRAC

*CENTRES OF STATION PLATFOR
RECORDED FOLLOWING A SUR
ALONG WESTBOUND CONDUCT
AND PLT/FMS USING A PEDOME
35mm GAIN OVER 10M TRA*

PADDINGTON STATION

1861·2 m

W.D.O. (RP) STATION

LOCO SIDING   SUB-STN (M/C FLOOR)

91·4m

91·4m

W.D.O.   908·9 m   727·7 m

MOUNT PLEASANT STATION

CATCH POINTS

W.C.D.O. 1376·0m

CAR DEPOT

LIVERPOOL ST. STATION

91·4m

91·4m

91·4m

K.E.B.   1312·3 m   17:

| ☐ SUB STATION | Ⓒ CABIN | Ⓒ CHUTE | Ⓛ LIFT (No1 etc) | SH |
| | CS CHUTE & STAIRS | Ⓢ STAIRS | Ⓑ BAG ELEVATOR | VR |

124

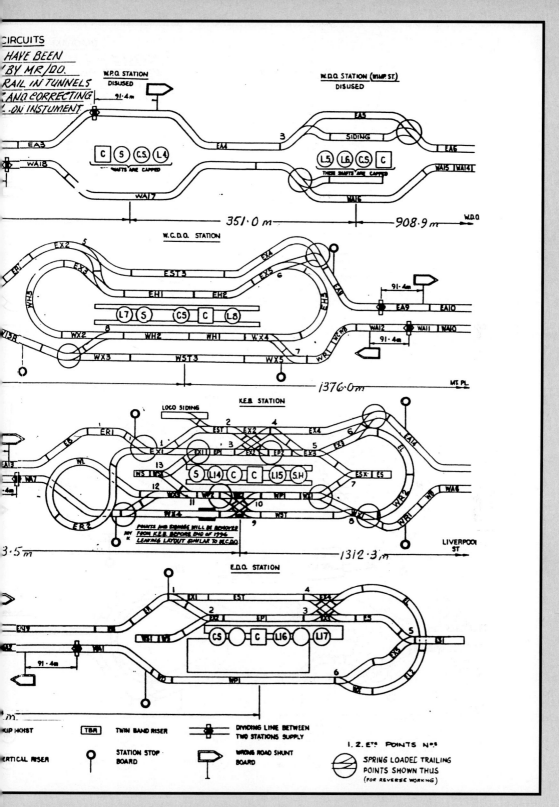

Track diagram, as in 1995. *Peter Johnson Collection*

Museum in Sussex. It was initially expected that the old stock would be withdrawn, but 16 units remain in service, giving a total operating fleet of 50 units. Twenty five units are stored out of use at various locations on the railway.

In 1986 a Post Office survey showed that the railway could still transfer mail in London for up to 40% less than the cost of the equivalent road transport. The following year the railway's 60th anniversary coincided with the fitting of 'aerodynamic' covers to three of the cars, over the power units mounted at each end, in anticipation that the covers would improve performance in the tunnels and keep the power units cleaner; no other vehicles were so modified. At the same time the railway, always called 'The Post Office Railway (London)' became known as 'Mail Rail'. Projects to centralise control with computerisation and to build a branch to Farringdon, to connect with Thameslink inter-Regional trains were also announced. The latter would have been a single-line tube connected to both Mount Pleasant and King Edward Building, creating a triangular junction which would allow trains to go either east or west. At the same time it was suggested that a further branch could be built between Paddington and Kensington if traffic built up sufficiently.

The control centralisation project was completed in 1993. The 1927 electro-mechanical system had continued to work satisfactorily but needed high manning levels; replacement parts were difficult to source and often had to be custom-made. Vaughan Systems of Ware supplied the new system costing £750,000. The computer system controls the railway from a central console at Mount Pleasant. It shows the position of every train on the system and can be operated manually or automatically. The control centre is operated by three traffic controllers who cover the

railway's 5½-day (13.00-08.00) operating period with shifts of 12.00-22.00, 20.00-04.00 and 23.00-09.00. Sunday evening working, the half day, will finish in October 1996.

The stations have their own local control computer, interfacing to the existing relays. The new system was installed at the rate of one station per week, the changeover taking place at weekends, without any disruption to services or parallel running. Except for those at Mount Pleasant, left to show visitors, the old diagrams and lever frames were removed.

A proposal to build a branch to the Willesden Hub was evaluated but failed because it could not be justified financially over a 10-year period. The Hub's existence will have an effect on the railway, for the Paddington-Liverpool Street traffic will transfer to it from 1996, bringing with it the closure of Liverpool Street Mail Rail station.

In August 1994 the Western District Office was merged with the WC District Office, the latter then ceasing to be manned, although continuing in use as a holding site for trains *en route* to WDO at busy times. In 1996 the merger of London Chief Office (King Edward Building) with Mount Pleasant will cause the closure of the former station. These changes, which will see the railway reduced to one of only four stations, and five closed ones, will be made in pursuit of efficiency and quality of service improvements. Rail Mail's day will come, however, if serious restrictions are placed on the use of road vehicles in central London.

Below: **1982-built unit No 32 is one of the streamlined cars. Named *City of London*, it has the City's crest on the front; when photographed on 14 June 1995 the plates had been removed.**
Peter Johnson

Bibliography

BOOKS AND MAGAZINES

Anon; *Life on the TPO A 'strictly unofficial' account by a seasoned traveller;* TPO Joint Production Committee, 1972

Bayliss, Derek A.; *The Post Office Railway London;* Turntable Publications, 1978

Carter, W. G.; *The Post Office (London) Railway;* General Post Office (Green Paper No 36), 1937

Cormack, John; 'Mail by Rail into the next decade'; *Railway Magazine,* April, 1994

'Finetuning the Postal Services'; *Modern Railways,* April 1995

Goodbody, A. M.; *An introduction and guide to the Travelling Post Offices of Great Britain;* Railway Philatelic Group, 2nd Edition, 1983

Haram, V. S.; *Centenary of the Irish Mail 1848-1948;* Railway Executive, London Midland Region, 1948

Harvey, A. M.; *Travelling Post Offices, Bag Tenders etc of Great Britain and Ireland from 1838;* unpublished manuscript, 1960

Hendy, J. G.; *History of the Travelling Post Offices compiled from official records;* unpublished manuscript, 1905

Below: **Loading at the London Chief Office, King Edward Building, in January 1988. The through line is on the right.** *Peter Johnson*

Hendy, J. G.; *History of the mail bag exchange apparatus compiled from official records;* unpublished manuscript, 1905

Hill, Geoffrey; *The Worsdells — A Quaker Engineering Dynasty;* Transport Publishing Co, 1991

Hill, Norman; *TPO postmarks of the British Isles;* Author, 1962

Hill, Norman; *The Railway Travelling Post Offices of Great Britain and Ireland 1838-1975;* Harry Hayes, 1977

Hosegood, J. G.; *Great Western Railway Travelling Post Offices;* Wild Swan Publications Ltd, 1983

Johnson, Peter; *The British Travelling Post Office;* Ian Allan, 1985

Johnson, Peter; *'Travelling Post Offices — The first 150 years'; Railway World,* October 1988

List of Travelling Post Offices, Sorting Carriages and mail bag duties; General Post Office, 1926

Obradovic, A.; *The TPO network, notes for a lecture;* presented to the Chartered Institute of Transport (Western Section), 1984

Obradovic, A.; *The Management of the Travelling Post Offices of Great Britain Historical Notes;* unpublished manuscript, revised 1994

Obradovic, A.; *The Travelling Post Office;* unpublished manuscript, 1994

The Post Office Railway (London); GPO, 1936 and several subsequent editions

Rowden, J. J. C.; *The Travelling Post Office;* General Post Office (Green Paper No 24), 1936

Royal Mail Travelling Post Offices TPO Initiative '91 information for TPO staff; TPO Section, 1991

Rules for Working Lineside Mail Apparatus; HMSO, 1939 and 1962

Rules for Officers of Travelling Post Offices; HMSO, 1955

Stubbs, R. M. & Roberts, G. P.; *TPO Postmarks of Great Britain 1962-1990;* TPO & Seapost Society, 1991

The Story of the Travelling Post Office; The Post Office, 1991

The TPO Handbook — your guide to all the changes including phase 1 and phase 2; The Post Office, 1988

The TPO Review — phase 1 — The TPO Changes and You; The Post Office, 1988

TPO — The story of the Travelling Post Office; The Post Office, 1988

Ward, C. W.; *English TPOs — Their history and postmarks;* Author, 1949

Ward, C. W.; *Irish TPOs — Their history and postmarks;* Author, 1938

Ward, C. W.; *Scottish TPOs — Their history and postmarks;* Author, 1947

Wilson, Frank J.; *Great Britain & Ireland Travelling Post Office Postmarks, a guide and catalogue;* Railway Philatelic Group, 1991

Wilson, H. S.; *TPO — A history of the Travelling Post Offices of Great Britain Part 1 England — The Specials and associated TPOs;* Railway Philatelic Group. 3rd Edition, 1979

Wilson, H. S.; *TPO — A history of the Travelling Post Offices of Great Britain Part 2 England — South of the Midland TPO;* Railway Philatelic Group, 2nd Edition, 1979

Wilson, H. S.; *TPO — A history of the Travelling Post Offices of Great Britain Part 3 Scotland and Ireland;* Railway Philatelic Group, 1977

PUBLICATIONS ON ROLLING STOCK

Andred; 'Post Office push-pull'; *Modern Railways,* October 1993

Casserley, R. M. & Millard, P. A.; *A Register of West Coast Joint Stock;* Historical Model Railway Society, 1980

Ellis, C. H.; *Railway Carriages in the British Isles 1830-1914;* Allen & Unwin, 1965

Essery, R. J. & Jenkinson, D.; *The LMS Coach;* Ian Allan, 1969

Gould, David; *Carriage Stock of the SECR;* Oakwood, 1976

Gould, David; *Maunsell's SR Steam Passenger Stock 1923-1939;* Oakwood, 1978

Harris, Michael; *Great Western Coaches;* David St John Thomas Publisher, 1993

Harris, Michael; *LNER Carriages*; David St John Thomas Publisher, 1994

Harris, Michael; *Preserved Railway Coaches;* Ian Allan, 1976

Hunter, D. L. G.; *Carriages & Waggons of the Highland Railway;* Turntable Enterprises, 1971

Kidner, R. W.; *Service Stock of the Southern Railway;* Oakwood, 1980

Larkin, David; *BR General Parcels Rolling Stock — A pictorial survey*; D. Bradford Barton, 1978

Lloyd, John & Brown, Murray; *Preserved Railway Carriages;* Silver Link Publishing, 1992

Mountford, E. R.; *A Register of GWR Absorbed Stock;* Oakwood, 1978

Newbury, P. J.; *Carriage Stock of the London, Brighton & South Coast Railway;* Oakwood, 1975.

Parkin, Keith; *British Railway Mark 1 Coaches;* Pendragon Books/Historical Model Railway Society, 1991

PERIODICALS

Railway Philately; the journal of the Railway Philatelic Group, 1966 to date

The Traveller; the journal of the TPO branch, Union of Post Office Workers, 1946-52

TPO; the journal of the TPO & Seapost Society, 1947 to date